CALIFORNIA'S
Eastern Sierra
A VISITOR'S GUIDE

By Sue Irwin

Cachuma Press

Published in Cooperation with the Eastern Sierra Interpretive Association

Editor: John Evarts
Designer: Adine Maron
Associate Editor: Marjorie Popper
Editorial Assistants: Katey O'Neill, Cynthia
Anderson
Cartography: Susan Kuromiya
Map Illustration: Linda Trujillo
Charts: John Evarts
Typesetting: Graphic Traffic

Published in cooperation with the Eastern Sierra
Interpretive Association.

Printed and bound in Hong Kong.

Library of Congress Cataloging-in-Publication
Data
Irwin, Sue.
    California's eastern Sierra : a visitor's guide /
by Sue Irwin.
       p.   cm.
    "Published in cooperation with the Eastern
Sierra Interpretive Association."
    Includes bibliographical references and index.
    ISBN 0-9628505-0-0
    1. Sierra Nevada Mountains (Calif. and
Nev.)—Description and travel—Guide-books.
I. Eastern Sierra Interpretive Association.
II. Title.
F868.S5I79   1991
917.94 ' 40453—dc20   91-23106
                    CIP

ACKNOWLEDGEMENTS
    We thank the many people who read portions of the manuscript. The insights, comments, and
suggestions you provided were invaluable to this project. For her thoughtful review and critique of the
text at key stages of its development, we are especially grateful to Carolyn Lynch. Her knowledge of the
Eastern Sierra and familiarity with its natural features were indispensable in helping us produce a
popular guide to the region. We also extend a special thank you to Chris Mueller for her editorial
contributions; to Jacki Fromme for her wonderful enthusiasm and encouragement; and to KC Wylie for
her long-standing support of this publishing endeavor.
    We greatly appreciate the effort of the following individuals who assisted with information gathering,
fact-checking, or technical review: Dave Babb, Kathy Barnes, Vern Bleich, Alice Boothe, Dave Carle,
Mary DeDecker, Wymond Eckhardt, Bill Evarts, Melanie Findling, Larry Ford, Carole Gerard, Karl
Halbach, John Harris, Hal Kleforth, Molly McCartney, Vern McLean, Bill Michael, Dorothy Miller, Jim
Morefield, Pam Murphy, Erin O'Conner-Henry, Geraldine Pasqua, Mike Patterson, Bruce Pavlik, Gary
Pingle, Phil Pister, Joe Pollini, Mike Prather, Denyse Racine, Janet Rantz, Arlene Reveal, John Roupp,
Terry Russi, Howard Sheckter, Jack Shipley, Dave Swart, Jane Torgeson, Nancy Upham, John
Wehausen, Patti Wells, Darrel Wong, and Mark Ziegenbein. Thank you all.
                                                                    —John Evarts and Sue Irwin

    Material quoted on page 7 is from *A Natural History of Western Trees* by Donald Culross Peattie. ©
1950, 1951, and 1952 by Donald Culross Peattie. © Renewed 1981 by Noel Peattie. Reprinted with
permission of Houghton Mifflin Co.
    Material quoted on pages 15, 18, 65, and 75 is from *Up and Down California in 1860-1864* by William
H. Brewer. Edited/translated by Francis Farquhar. © 1949 by The Regents of the University of
California. Reprinted with permission of University of California Press.

Contents

*Cover: Owens Valley boulder gardens and Mt.
Williamson, near Independence.* CARR CLIFTON
*Title Spread: First light on Mt Whitney and the
Sierra skyline west of Lone Pine.* CARR CLIFTON
Above left: Dawn, Lone Pine Peak. CARR CLIFTON
Above: Sand dunes and tufa, Mono Lake. JEFF GNASS

Introduction

The vast acreage folded between the Sierra Nevada crest and the White-Inyo Range is so dramatic and infinitely varied that some people wonder why it is not a national park. Few places on the planet offer a greater collage of unspoiled environments in so small an area: everything from blistering hot deserts to sighing pine forests to 14,000-foot granite crags, hung with glaciers and flanked by icy lakes. Crowned by the Sierra's imposing eastern escarpment, this is a land of both subtlety and extremes, a place that sings to the bottom layers of our souls.

I was lucky enough to be born in the long shadows of the Owens Valley, where I grew up tramping mountain trails with the Boy Scouts, four-wheel driving with my parents, and screaming down Mammoth Mountain's exciting Cornice with teenage friends. This is where I learned to build a fire, catch fish, rock climb, and navigate through mountain and desert wilderness—skills that would later prove invaluable as I traveled the world as a mountaineering guide and photojournalist. But no matter how uplifting the scenery elsewhere, I am always drawn back home to the Eastern Sierra. This extraordinary landscape has shown me much about truth and beauty and continues to shape my perceptions about the world.

Like many who live here, I used to want to keep this whole part of California a secret. Ten years ago, I would have hated this book more than politicians hate leaks. But how selfish, how shortsighted! Not only do visitors and tourists fuel an otherwise desiccated economy, many also leave with a new appreciation of the natural wonders this wild environment still reveals. The region needs this constituency for its very survival.

Given the harsh realities of our overcrowded planet, it is astonishing that this huge, underpopulated watershed hasn't already been "discovered" and carved up for a variety of manmade schemes. Ironically, much credit for preservation of the Eastern Sierra's wide open spaces goes to the City of Los Angeles, whose Department of Water and Power bought most of Owens Valley to supply the city with water. Most other acreage here is public land, administered by the Forest Service or Bureau of Land Management. There simply isn't enough private land to build many new houses, farms, or factories.

We all occasionally need to see a wild and sweeping horizon just to keep from going crazy, and perhaps nowhere else so close to a city are there more spectacular panoramas than in the Eastern Sierra. As California's population continues to mushroom, the value of this region's untrammeled open space will steadily grow. Each year, more and more motorists head up Highway 395, discovering that every turn and sideroad brings a different view, some steeped in rough-and-tumble history, others beckoning to hikers, rock climbers, artists, or anglers. If only the Eastern Sierra can remain unscarred by new cities, roads, power lines, and water diversion schemes, its scenery alone might bring far more life to the area's economy than all the boom-and-bust mining, ranching, and hydroelectric power the region has ever produced.

I like this book not only because it will help readers learn more about a landscape that badly needs stronger protection, but also because it introduces many unique destinations even most locals have overlooked. Its pages resonate with possibilities for exploration and discovery—something all too rare in the rest of the world. Sue Irwin has walked, driven, skied, and climbed long miles checking out the special places she describes. The result is a detailed and sensitive guide that will help many visitors gain a deeper appreciation of this national park that isn't.

—*Gordon Wiltsie*
March, 1991

Left: Western bristlecone pines in the Patriarch Grove, White Mountains. DAVID MUENCH

Natural History of the Eastern Sierra

The great mountain wall of the Sierra Nevada has two unlike faces. The western face, intercepting the moisture-laden winds from the Pacific, is well watered, and magnificently forested, and though the descent from the highest peaks to the base is great, the angle of the slope is not. In absolute contrast is the eastern face of this range of mountains. It forms, in places, one of the steepest, swiftest descents—almost a downward plunge—of the planet's surface. It faces the desert, and its slopes are arid. At first this side of the Sierra appears much the less hospitable and charming, and it is certainly less accessible. But in time one comes to have a special affection for its dramatic scenery, for its pure, cold lakes so secretively concealed, for the bracing dryness of its air, for its greater wildness and lack of milling throngs of our fellow humans.

—Donald Culross Peattie,
A Natural History of Western Trees, 1953

Left: Foxtail pine, a hardy conifer that grows in the Sierra high country. ANDY SELTERS
Opposite: Sand dunes and volcanic rock above Owens Lake playa, looking north up the deep trough of Owens Valley. DAVID MUENCH

Desolation Lake and Mt. Humphreys in the John Muir Wilderness west of Bishop. PAT O'HARA

A Land of Dramatic Contrasts

The Eastern Sierra is vast, rugged, and sparsely populated. It is a land of dramatic contrasts and remarkable beauty, a place where the juxtaposition of mountain and desert environments produces breathtaking scenery and fascinating natural history. Glacier-scoured peaks tower above shimmering alkali flats; rippling sand dunes lie in the rain shadow of 14,000-foot summits; snow-fed mountain streams tumble through coniferous forests, flowing toward arid basins that have no outlet to the sea.

This landscape is the meeting place of the Sierra Nevada, the Great Basin, and the Mojave Desert. Their geology, climates, flora, and fauna intermingle here, creating a rich collage of natural communities. Not only is the Eastern Sierra diverse, it also claims a number of unparalleled features: Mount Whitney, the tallest peak in the contiguous United States; Inyo Volcanic Chain, one of the youngest volcanic regions in the country; Palisade Glacier, the southernmost active glacier in the United States; Mono Lake, one of the oldest bodies of water in existence on our continent; and western bristlecone pines, the world's oldest continuously living organisms.

Although a technical definition of "eastern Sierra" would include the entire length of the Sierra Nevada, it is the high country south of Sonora Pass—as well as the desert valleys and mountains to the immediate east of the range—that are popularly considered the Eastern Sierra. The heart of the region extends along the east slope of the range, from Mount Whitney to Yosemite National Park. This 125-mile stretch is the highest and wildest section of the Sierra; the crest here averages 12,000 feet, forming an awesome mountain wall capped by many of California's tallest peaks. Four large basins—Owens Valley, Long Valley, Mono Basin, and Bridgeport Valley—are located along the base of the Sierra's steep eastern escarpment. They are home to most of the area's population and are connected by U.S. 395, the only major highway in the region. The Eastern Sierra also encompasses the White-Inyo Range. These high, arid mountains parallel the Sierra for over 100 miles, and are most accessible from Owens Valley.

Dynamic Geology

The Eastern Sierra's geologic features are magnificent and diverse. They have figured prominently in the region's cultural history, from Paiute legends, to prospector's tales of lost mines, to the dispute over the naming of Mount Whitney. From the time it was first described in the journals of 19th-century visitors such as William Brewer, Clarence King, and John Muir, this landscape has fascinated geologists and nature lovers. Muir summed it up well when he exalted: "A country of wonderful contrasts. Hot deserts bounded by snow-laden mountains,—cinders and ashes scattered on glacier-polished pavements,—frost and fire working together in the making of beauty."

In contrast to the gently ascending, forested slopes of the western Sierra, the east side is arid, steep, and seemingly stark. Unobstructed by dense vegetation, landforms are easy to see, accessible, and often visible for great distances in the dry desert air. To the immediate east of the Sierra Nevada, Owens Valley comprises an abundance of geologic sites; its sand dunes, lava fields, cinder cones, fault scarps, and ancient lake shores are evidence of a remarkable geologic heritage. The valley itself is bounded by two of the highest ranges in the United States: the Sierra Nevada and the White-Inyo Range. Further north, the Mammoth-Mono region encompasses an equally dramatic lanscape. Everywhere there is evidence of the work of fire and ice. Glacier-excavated canyons open onto basins and valleys that cradle lava domes, craters, volcanoes, and hot springs— reminders of the Eastern Sierra's dynamic geology.

Plate Tectonics and the Sierra Batholith

Geologists rely on the concept of plate tectonics to understand the complex

Looking north along the Sierra crest from Mt. Langley; Owens Valley is at the upper right. DAVID MUENCH

processes of mountain-building that have shaped the Eastern Sierra. This theory proposes that the earth's crust, rather than being a continuous shell, is made up of segments or plates that move about over the planet's molten interior. Earth scientists believe the core of the Sierra Nevada began forming about 225 million years ago as a result of a major collision between two tectonic plates. Up until that time, the landscape we now call the Eastern Sierra was a relatively flat plane beneath a shallow sea that extended across present-day Nevada.

From about 225 to 65 million years ago, the edge of the eastward-moving Pacific Plate repeatedly dived beneath the westward-drifting North American Plate, causing plumes of magma (molten rock) to periodically rise from great depths. The magma slowly cooled and crystallized a few miles below the earth's surface, solidifying into a coarse-grained rock. These intrusions of magma, known as plutons, formed the vast granitic cores, or batholiths, that underlie the Sierra Nevada, White Mountains, and several other California ranges.

as the Basin Ranges; of these, the westernmost is the White-Inyo Range, which rises to the east of Owens Valley and crests at over 14,000 feet.

Faults and Earthquakes

The Sierra Nevada and White-Inyo Range are called fault-block ranges because they are formed of huge, uplifted blocks of earth bounded by faults (fractures in the earth's crust). During various episodes of mountain-building, faults developed at the base of the ranges. Intense seismic activity in fault zones along the east side of the Sierra thrust the mountain block skyward and tilted it to the west, producing a range with a gentle western slope and a breathtakingly steep eastern escarpment.

As the two ranges were pushed upward, the land that lay between the mountains' parallel faults dropped downward. This action helped form the deep trough, or graben, which is now Owens Valley. Although the valley boasts more than 10,000 feet of vertical relief both to the east and west, the combined effect of uplifting and downdropping along the faults is even more dramatic than it appears: the bedrock of Owens Valley, at one time level with the rock of surrounding peaks, is now buried beneath at least 6,000 feet of debris and sediment. The shift along the faults, then, has been over 16,000 feet—three vertical miles!

Prior to the uplift that produced the modern-day Sierra, the region experienced several major episodes of mountain-building and erosion. An entire pre-Sierran range, estimated to reach over 10,000 feet, was thrust up and then subsequently worn down, as weathering and erosion reduced it to low, rolling hills. The most recent period of uplift began within the last 10 million years and formed the towering range we see today. Over 400 miles long and averaging 50 to 80 miles wide, the Sierra Nevada is one of the highest and largest mountain ranges in the contiguous United States. Its granitic batholith, exposed by uplift and erosion and later scoured by ice-age glaciers, imparts a unique grandeur to the range John Muir called "the most divinely beautiful of all."

The Great Basin, directly east of the Sierra, was also uplifted in response to tectonic stress. This mountain-building process resulted in the formation of the Basin and Range region, an area that sprawls over several western states and encompasses hundreds of parallel, north-south trending ranges and basins. The mountains are collectively referred to

The Sierra Nevada continues to rise. Measurements indicate that in places the range is being uplifted at the rate of 2 inches every 10 years. As with most geologic processes, the movements are usually too slow and subtle for us to notice, but sensitive seismic instruments record frequent, small earthquakes in the area. Movements along Eastern Sierra faults have also produced some powerful temblors. In 1872 a catastrophic earthquake leveled the town of Lone Pine and set off avalanches in distant Yosemite Valley. During that single event, the vertical displacement along the fault was, in places, nearly 17 feet. Mammoth Lakes was struck by a less destructive earthquake in May 1980. The temblor registered 6.1 on the Richter Scale and was followed by over 600 aftershocks that rumbled through the area for two months.

Volcanism

The tectonic stresses that build mountains also give rise to volcanic activity. Volcanism occurs when magma moves upward from deep reservoirs and breaches the earth's crust. Faults sometimes provide avenues along which magma moves to the surface, and in the Eastern Sierra there are over 50 extinct or dormant volcanoes found along fault zones. Craters, cinder cones, lava domes, lava flows, and boiling hot springs are among the many volcanic features that attest to the area's geologic vigor.

The Mammoth-Mono region, with the youngest chain of lava domes and craters in the United States, still holds the promise of continued volcanic activity. Indeed, the earthquakes of 1980 were associated with possible magmatic activity. The largest existing volcano of Inyo and Mono counties is Mammoth Mountain, which was active between 180,000 and 40,000 years ago. Since steam occasionally rises from fumaroles (vents) near its summit, the volcano is considered dormant rather than extinct.

Glaciation

More than any other agent of nature, the work of glaciers has shaped the Sierra and contributed to the beauty and drama of the mountain landscape. During the ice ages of the Pleistocene, vast glaciers developed in the Sierra high country. Cycles of cooling and warming, occurring between 1 million and 10,000 years ago, brought at least six episodes of glacial advance and retreat to the range.

During these ice ages, when cooler temperatures and heavy precipitation prevailed, winter snows failed to melt completely during summer months. As a result, snowfields grew larger and deeper year after year, until their sheer weight compacted and transformed old snow into glacial ice. Eventually yielding to the tug of gravity, the glaciers became great

Above: Negit Island in Mono Lake is about 1,700 years old and considered a young volcano. WILLIAM NEILL

Opposite: The Sierra's steep eastern face formed as the range was uplifted and tilted west; at the same time, basins along fault zones east of the mountains dropped down. WILLIAM NEILL

Top: Palisade Glacier west of Big Pine, the largest in the Sierra Nevada. DAVID MUENCH
Bottom: Sparsely covered desert slopes are easily eroded, such as this canyon in the Inyo Mountains east of Lone Pine. BILL EVARTS

rivers of ice flowing slowly downhill, quarrying out steep cirques, stair-step lake basins, and U-shaped valleys.

As they moved downhill, glaciers plucked boulders from the bedrock and picked up loose material that collected on the sides, fell on top, or was carried within the descending ice. The glacier-transported rubble was revealed as the climate warmed and the ice melted back. Ridges of debris, known as glacial moraines, formed along the borders and at the terminus of a glacier's path. Terminal moraines, often dating from several episodes of glacial advance, are visible near the mouths of most Sierra canyons from Independence north. The Pleistocene glaciers that sculpted the Sierra have all disappeared. The small glaciers we see today, such as Palisade Glacier above Big Pine Canyon, are remnants of a minor period of glaciation that occurred within the last 4,000 years.

While glaciers have scoured much of the Sierra, they have not played a major role in the geologic history of the White-Inyo Range. Although the White Mountains are nearly as high as the Sierra Nevada, they are far more arid; during ice ages, they lacked the volume of precipitation necessary to form large glaciers.

Weathering and Erosion

The work of weathering can be witnessed throughout the Eastern Sierra. Agents of physical weathering—water, ice, and wind— are continually shaping the terrain. Where air and water react with the minerals in rocks to break them down, chemical weathering also plays a role. The brown, rounded boulders of the Alabama Hills, for example, were at one time jointed blocks of hard, whitish granite; their edges have been gradually rounded by chemical weathering and their surfaces stained by the oxidation of iron minerals in the rock. Although both ranges are subjected to similar forces of weathering, the jagged profile of the Sierra contrasts markedly with the softer contours of the White-Inyo Range. The Sierra owes its sharp, chiselled features and sawtooth ridges to its jointed granite; as water repeatedly freezes, thaws, expands, and refreezes in the joints, it weakens and eventually fractures the rock. The softer sedimentary rock that caps much of the White-Inyo Range lacks the extensive jointing that makes the Sierra's granite so vulnerable to ice-driven fracture.

Much of the Eastern Sierra receives little rain, and vegetation that helps anchor soil and rock is sparse. When rain does fall, it often comes in short, intense storms that efficiently erode the mountains. Fast-moving, short-lived streams form, sweeping any loose material down narrow canyons. These intermittent streams deposit their loads of silt, rocks, and boulders at the bases of the canyons, creating fan-shaped slopes called alluvial fans. Typical of desert ranges, alluvial fans are found on both sides of Owens Valley and are most prominent below steep canyons in the White-Inyo Range and Sierra Nevada.

The process of erosion eventually carries alluvial materials downslope to basins and valley bottoms. The surface of Owens Valley, for example, sits atop a mile-deep accumulation of alluvium. Where strong winds regularly rake across sparsely covered areas, particles of sand are picked up and bounced along the desert floor. Over time, these wind-propelled particles pile up against barriers such as ridges or swaths of vegetation to form sand dunes. The Eastern Sierra's best-developed dunes are located south of Owens Lake, a few miles east of Olancha.

Rocks and Minerals

Igneous rock, in the form of granite, is dominant in the Sierra Nevada; striking examples of granite are seen along virtually every sideroad that ascends the eastern escarpment. The oldest rock in the range is metamorphic; it began as sedimentary sea-floor deposits and was later altered by intense heat and pressure (metamorphism) during periods of magmatic intrusion. As the range was uplifted, the overlying metamorphic layer was elevated, tilted, and folded.

The Alabama Hills' weathered blocks of granite were at one time covered by alluvial deposits. BILL EVARTS

The Sierra's cap of metamorphic rock, once thousands of feet deep, has largely been stripped away by erosion, revealing the granite beneath. The gray and rusty-red hues of metamorphic rock are still visible, however, especially in peaks west of Bishop and Crowley Lake.

Sedimentary rock is prevalent in the geologically complex White-Inyo Range. The White Mountains straddle a granitic batholith similar to the Sierra's; the granite, however, is exposed only on the northernmost summits of the range. The White

Mountains' 500- to 600-million-year-old sedimentary formations are among the oldest in California.

Igneous volcanic rock is the youngest rock in the region and is widespread in the basins and valleys east of the Sierra. Lava fields border U.S. 395 near Little Lake and Big Pine. Another product of volcanism is Bishop tuff, a type of rhyolite that formed as ash and gas fused together during the Long Valley eruption about 700,000 years ago; the tuff covers the sprawling Volcanic Tableland north of Bishop. Two forms of volcanic glass,

Pleistocene glaciers scoured and polished the top of Devils Postpile's columns of basalt. LARRY ULRICH

obsidian and pumice, are common in the Mammoth-Mono Region. The best-known volcanic rocks of the Eastern Sierra are the hexagonal columns of basalt at Devils Postpile National Monument, a geologic site that attracts over 100,000 visitors a year.

A number of valuable minerals are found in the Eastern Sierra, including gold, silver, lead, zinc, and tungsten. During various mountain-building episodes, the overlying rock developed fractures and faults in response to geologic stress. These fractures were filled by mineral solutions, such as gold-bearing quartz, during subsequent periods of magmatic intrusion. The discovery of veins of gold and silver during the 1860s and 1870s at locations such as Cerro Gordo, Kearsarge, Bodie, Lundy, and Mammoth attracted successive waves of emigrants and changed the course of human history in the Eastern Sierra.

Climate

As recently as 10,000 years ago, the Eastern Sierra environment was far different from the one we see today. The climate was more moist, and abundant precipitation and run-off sustained a dense vegetative cover. Prehistoric mammoths, camels, mastodons, and horses roamed the land. Mono Basin and lower Owens

As air passes over the Sierra during winter, it oscillates between cold and warm temperature layers, creating cloud "waves." GORDON WILTSIE

Valley were filled by enormous lakes. A glacial river flowed southward between the Sierra Nevada and the White-Inyo Range, carving a path through basins, valleys, and lava fields. But as the last ice age came to a close, the climate began to change; the weather grew warmer and drier, and the lush landscape gradually became a semi-desert.

Today's arid climate most closely resembles that of the Great Basin. The region's salient meteorological characteristics include wide temperature swings between day and night and from winter to summer; relatively low humidity year-round; annual precipitation totals below 12 inches in most valleys; warm to very hot summer days, occasionally punctuated by thunderstorms; low nighttime temperatures in winter; and mild spring and fall weather, especially at lower elevations.

Owens Valley is the warmest and most arid portion of the Eastern Sierra. Its weather, like its flora and fauna, reflects the influence of the Mojave Desert. Summers are hot, winters are mild, and rainfall averages less than six inches per year. To the north, Eastern Sierra summers are more moderate, and annual precipitation is greater, often falling as snow. Some of California's lowest temperatures are recorded in the northern basins of the Eastern Sierra. In Bridgeport, for example, the average low temperature during January is 9°F.

In a landscape characterized by great differences in elevation, extraordinary gradients in temperature often occur over short distances. During July, typical midday temperatures hover near 100°F on the floor of Owens Valley at Lone Pine, elevation 3,700 feet; a 14-mile, 25-minute drive takes you to Whitney Portal, elevation 8,371 feet, where daytime temperatures are usually 20° cooler. The remarkable proximity of alpine and desert climates is one of the great natural attractions of the Eastern Sierra and has long intrigued visitors to the region. After leading the field party of the California State Geological Survey through Owens Valley on July 29, 1864, William Brewer wrote:

> It was a terrible day. The thermometer ranged from 102° to 106°, often the latter, and most of the time 104°.
>
> During this day's ride the Sierra loomed up grandly. The crest is at the extreme eastern part of the chain—grand rocky peaks . . . their cool snow, often apparently not over ten miles from us, mocking our heat.

The Sierra Rain Shadow

The mountain wall of the Sierra exerts a profound influence over the weather and is responsible for the region's aridity. Because of its tremendous height, the range casts a huge "rain shadow" that falls across the Eastern Sierra and extends far out into the Great Basin. Moisture-laden air masses that form over the northern Pacific Ocean between November and April are the primary source of precipitation in the Sierra. When they encounter the range, Pacific storm clouds are forced upward, dropping most of their water as they ascend the western slopes. By the time weather fronts arrive on the east side, the clouds have left most of their moisture behind.

Autumn showers west of Bishop, a welcome sight in this arid landscape. GALEN ROWELL / MOUNTAIN LIGHT

Depending on latitude and elevation, the west side of the Sierra receives between 20 and 80 inches of precipitation annually. With the exception of the high country near the Sierra crest, the eastern escarpment records only 5 to 20 inches per year. Moving east from the Sierra crest, the climate gets drier, except for the western slopes of the White-Inyo Range, which receive more rain than Owens Valley. The wettest part of the Eastern Sierra is found near Mammoth Pass where a low point in the crest allows moist Pacific storms to funnel through to the east side. This extra precipitation endows Mammoth Mountain Ski Area with an annual average of 335 inches of snow and sustains a belt of coniferous forest that extends farther downslope than in any other location along the east side.

Not all of the Eastern Sierra's precipitation comes from Pacific winter storms. Ellery Lake above Lee Vining, for example, receives an average of 1.5 inches of rain each summer—virtually all from thundershowers. On hot summer afternoons, especially when moist subtropical air from northern Mexico and the Gulf of California has circulated into the Great Basin, towering thunderheads boil up over the mountains. Often accompanied by lightning and gusty winds, summer thunderstorms usually unleash short-lived torrents of rain or hail. In desert areas, intense cloudbursts occasionally trigger flash floods that wash out roads and inundate low-lying terrain. In August 1989, thunderstorms near Olancha set off debris flows that filled a two-mile stretch of the Los Angeles Aqueduct with boulders, sand, and mud.

Flora of the Eastern Sierra

> Looking up the canyon from the warm sunny edge of the Mono plain my morning ramble seems a dream, so great is the change in the vegetation and climate. . . . the sunshine is hot enough for palms. Yet the snow round the arctic gardens at the summit of the pass is plainly visible, only about four miles away, and between lie specimen zones of all the principal climates of the globe.
>
> —John Muir,
> *My First Summer in the Sierra*

Few regions in the United States encompass a range of flora comparable to the Eastern Sierra. Here, within a matter of miles, the vegetation changes from desert scrub to alpine tundra, with woodland, forest, and wetland communities sandwiched in between. The steep, high mountains that create such exciting topography are responsible for much of the region's plant diversity. Rapid transitions in elevation, sometimes spanning from 3,000 to 14,000 feet in less than 10

Jeffrey pine and aspen border an Eastern Sierra creek below Mt. Morrison. LARRY ULRICH

aerial miles, produce dramatic variations in temperature and rainfall. The flora reflects these climatic differences and is correspondingly diverse. Where else in North America does a 30-mile drive begin in a landscape with sand dunes and creosote bushes and climb to a montane setting of subalpine meadows and foxtail pine?

The Sierra rain shadow, which produces a steep gradient of yearly precipitation from west to east across the area, exerts a significant influence over plant distribution. The rain shadow is the key reason that plant communities at the same elevation in the Sierra Nevada and White-Inyo Range are usually so different.

The rich flora of the Eastern Sierra is also the product of an unusual geographic junction—the confluence of the Mojave Desert, Great Basin, and Sierra Nevada. Each region embraces a distinctive vegetation that extends over a large geographic area, and each region's flora covers some part of the Eastern Sierra. Lower Owens Valley vegetation is most closely affiliated with the Mojave Desert. The plants of the White-Inyo Range and the territory east of the Sierra from Bishop to Bridgeport are primarily Great Basin species. The flora on the east slope of the Sierra Nevada comprises species from throughout the range.

A comprehensive survey of Eastern Sierra plants has not been undertaken,

During summer, wildflowers erupt into bloom throughout the Eastern Sierra high country. CARR CLIFTON

but ongoing research suggests the total number of species exceeds 1,500. At least 700 species have been identified on the floor of Owens Valley, nearly 1,000 species are now known to grow in the White Mountains, and about 250 species have been documented at University of California's 136-acre Valentine Camp near Mammoth Lakes.

Plant Communities

Groups of plants adapted to similar temperatures, precipitation, types of soil, and other environmental factors often grow in fairly predictable associations known as plant communities; each community comprises a characteristic flora, has its own physical structure, and is distinguished by a number of key species. Most Eastern Sierra plant communities are readily identified by their key or indicator species. For example, Great Basin sagebrush scrub and Jeffrey pine forest, two of the region's more widespread communities, are dominated by Great Basin sagebrush and Jeffrey pine, respectively.

Many plants, particularly indicator species, are not limited to one community. Great Basin sagebrush dominates the community of the same name, but it is also an important component of other communities, such as pinyon-juniper woodland. Although plant communities lack rigid boundaries, overlap along community borders, and have species in common, each community provides a unique framework for "reading" the terrain. Individually, they reflect conditions at a given site; collectively, they are living expressions of diversity and change in the natural landscape.

With the exception of wetland vegetation, the distribution of Eastern Sierra plant communities is closely tied to elevation. Any trip from the desert into the mountains traverses a succession of vegetation types, each containing one or more plant communities. In general, scrub communities cover the basins and lower-elevation slopes, woodlands and forest communities are widespread at the middle elevations of the mountains, and alpine fell-fields are found in the high country above treeline. Regardless of elevation, much of the Eastern Sierra flora shares a common trait: the ability to survive in a landscape of extremes.

Describing the shrubs of Owens Valley in 1864, William Brewer wrote: "Marvels of vegetation, some of these species will stand a tropical heat and a winter's frosts; the drought of years does not kill them. . . ." In Eastern

Sierra scrub communities, perennials exhibit a variety of adaptations for desert survival, such as extensive root systems that capture infrequent rainfall and runoff, small leaves for conserving moisture, and light-colored hairs and waxy surfaces to help reflect intense summer heat. Some species are drought-deciduous, dropping their leaves during extended dry spells.

The annuals within the scrub communities are most apparent after wet winters. Annuals' seeds, which may lie dormant in times of drought, burst to life following seasonal rains; if precipitation is sufficient, the arid scrublands produce brilliant displays of wildflowers. The sidebar near the end of this chapter, "Wildflowers of the Eastern Sierra," introduces a selection of colorful regional wildflowers.

Although rainfall is more plentiful in the mountains and higher-elevation valleys, woodlands and forests nurtured by this extra moisture must still contend with poor rocky soils, steep slopes, and adverse weather. Pinyon-juniper woodland is one of the most characteristic plant communities of the Great Basin and covers vast acreage in the Eastern Sierra, particularly in the White-Inyo Range. Singleleaf pinyon and Utah juniper, the woodland's key species, can persist where there is little topsoil and yearly rainfall of only eight inches. The taller, more imposing conifers found in forest communities are adapted to the rigors of the Eastern Sierra in many ways: western bristlecone pine, for example, has a shallow, spreading root system that takes advantage of the White Mountains' thin, nutrient-poor soils; Jeffrey pine, which is both drought and cold tolerant, is well established in the porous, volcanic soils of the Mammoth-Mono region, an area where few other trees can grow; whitebark pine ranges to the upper limits of the Sierra treeline, often forming shrubby or prostrate thickets (known as krummholz) that can withstand gale-force winds.

Above treeline, which generally occurs near 11,000 feet, the climate is especially challenging for plant life. Only the most tenacious species—those typically found in alpine fell-field communities—can survive the arctic temperatures, fierce desiccating winds, cool summers, and nine-month winters that are common at these elevations. Vegetation of the alpine fell-fields is almost exclusively composed of perennials; the four- to seven-week growing season at this altitude is too short for most annuals. Characteristic plants of the alpine fell-

These verdant, alpine meadows in the John Muir Wilderness are snow-covered most of the year. PAT O'HARA

fields are small, compact, and low-growing; many are anchored to windswept sites by long roots that penetrate fractured rocks in search of soil and moisture.

In the arid Eastern Sierra, wetland vegetation is a reliable indicator of one of the region's most valuable resources—water. Riparian plant communities typically occur near springs and along the borders of creeks, rivers, and other watercourses. In desert areas, verdant streamside corridors can be spotted from miles away, delineated by narrow ribbons of greenery where creeks tumble past the sparse vegetation of scrub and woodland communities. Riparian communities also cut a distinctive path through forested areas; deciduous trees and shrubs such as black cottonwood, quaking aspen, water birch, and willow crowd the banks of creeks and other drainages, creating swaths of seasonal color amid the evergreens.

The floor of lower Owens Valley contains an unusual community known as the alkali sink wetland. For this plant community to exist, three major factors must converge: a near-surface water table; high heat and consequent evaporation, which prevents water from lingering at the surface after runoff accumulates; and a high salt content in the soil, which results from the wetland's rapid evaporation and closed drainage. The

plants that tolerate these salt-encrusted soils are "specialists" whose unusual physiologies have long intrigued botanists.

Wherever wetland vegetation is found, its importance in this semi-desert landscape cannot be overstated. Wetland communities help protect crucial watersheds, provide food, cover, and homes for wildlife, and usually occur in areas where

recreational activities such as fishing and camping are concentrated.

As you explore the Eastern Sierra, you may want to consult the table, "Major Plant Communities of the Eastern Sierra," located at the end of this chapter. This table introduces the region's plant communities, gives their general distribution, lists characteristic species, and provides sample locations where the communities are found.

Wetlands such as Fish Slough (shown) are a crucial habitat for wildlife in the arid Eastern Sierra. BILL EVARTS

Wildlife of the Eastern Sierra

A diverse population of wildlife inhabits the Eastern Sierra and is composed of animals characteristic of the Sierra Nevada, Great Basin, and Mojave Desert regions. The variety of habitats compressed into the Eastern Sierra's steep and varied topography allows for unusual combinations of wildlife; this is a landscape where black bears, California gulls, and desert horned lizards may be neighbors.

Every part of the region offers unique opportunities for viewing wildlife. Depending on the season, you can see sage grouse strutting and booming in Long Valley, watch bighorn sheep descending a steep Sierra canyon, spot a chuckwalla sunning on the lava at Fossil Falls, or glimpse a golden trout darting through the waters of Cottonwood Creek. In the preface to his book *Birds of Yosemite and the East Slope*, David Gaines describes conducting a tour of Mono Lake and shares an exciting moment of wildlife viewing:

Ten thousand phalaropes welcomed us to Mono's dominion. As the cameraman filmed, the birds exploded into flight, veering and diving as a Prairie Falcon cut through their midst.

That burst of wings and talons immersed us in a drama more vivid and real than anything on television or in a book. In some ineluctable way, the grace of those shorebirds, the power of that falcon, overpowered our preoccupied brains. No longer merely observers, we were swept by the flow of this living planet.

Mammals

More than 80 species of mammals are found in the Eastern Sierra. They occur in virtually every habitat, ranging from desert dunes to coniferous forests to alpine summits. A number of mammals, such as mule deer, coyote, and black-tailed jackrabbit, are relatively widespread. Others, such as bighorn sheep and pronghorn, were once common but their populations declined in the 20th century due to the impacts of commercial hunting, introduced diseases, and competition from domestic livestock. Bighorn sheep, which inhabit both the Sierra and White-Inyo Range, are the feature of the sidebar in Chapter Five, "Bighorn Sheep in the Eastern Sierra."

Pronghorn, the swiftest mammal in North America, had disappeared from the Eastern Sierra by the 1930s. This graceful animal, which stands about three feet high at the shoulders, is often mistakenly referred to as an antelope; the pronghorn, however, is unique to this continent and is not

Top: Mule deer are widespread in the Eastern Sierra, and large herds overwinter in the region's high-desert valleys. DENNIS FLAHERTY
Bottom: Pronghorn, the fastest mammals in N. America, have been reintroduced to their native range in the Eastern Sierra. FRED EBERT

Top: The yellow-bellied marmot is a high-country resident of the Sierra and is often seen near wilderness trailheads. KENNAN WARD
Bottom: Sierra bighorn rams. JOHN D. WEHAUSEN

closely related to the true antelopes of Africa and Central Asia. Once numbering in the millions and concentrated in the northern Great Plains, pronghorn are now numerous only in several western states that offer the wide open spaces they require. They were first reintroduced to the Eastern Sierra in 1949; the animals were to be released in Adobe Valley near Benton, but they broke out of a Department of Fish and Game truck at Bridgeport and eventually made their way to the Bodie Hills. During the 1980s, wildlife biologists from the Bureau of Land Management and Department of Fish and Game transplanted more pronghorn to the region. There are more than 200 pronghorn in the Eastern Sierra today, and their numbers are slowly expanding. The best location for viewing them is the Bodie Hills.

Among the Eastern Sierra's other colorful mammals are two nonnative species introduced from other regions of California: tule elk and beaver. A small herd of tule elk was imported to Owens Valley in 1933, and it eventually swelled into a population which now comprises about 500 individuals. (See the sidebar in Chapter Four, "Tule Elk of Owens Valley.") Beaver, not to be confused with the small native rodent known as mountain beaver (*Aplodontia rufa*), were first released in several Mono County streams in the 1940s; today,

beaver ponds and lodges can be spotted along Owens River and many east side creeks.

As year-round residents, mammals must adapt to the climatic rigors of the Eastern Sierra. Mountain-dwelling species employ various strategies to contend with winter's harsh weather and scarcity of food. Marmots, chipmunks, and ground squirrels fatten up during summer and early fall and retreat to underground dens to hibernate. Black bears also retire to dens, where they pass the winter in a lethargic, semi-dormant state that resembles hibernation. Deer mice, bushy-tailed woodrats, pikas, and chickarees gather and store extra food for winter; they spend the cold-weather months in protected burrows or nests, occasionally venturing out to retrieve cached provisions. Some mammals, such as pine martens, white-tailed jackrabbits, and bighorn sheep, are better equipped to withstand the cold and actively forage throughout the winter.

At lower elevations, mammals must cope with summer heat and dehydration. Many residents of the desert scrub have lighter colored coats than their mountain counterparts, an adaptation that presumably helps them reflect heat. Nocturnal mammals, such as woodrats, mice, and bats, avoid the heat because they rest during the day and forage during the cooler hours of evening and nighttime. Other mammals, such as coyotes and rabbits, escape the midday sun by resting in the shade or withdrawing to underground burrows. A few desert-dwellers, such as Mojave ground squirrels, spend the summer months in a kind of hot-weather hibernation known as estivation. Arid-climate residents with highly specialized metabolisms, such as kangaroo rats, antelope ground squirrels, and black-tailed jackrabbits, do not need to travel great distances for water because they derive moisture from their diet of seeds, grasses, and foliage.

Two of the Eastern Sierra's largest mammals, mule deer and bighorn sheep, are known to migrate over a great range of elevations in response to weather and seasonal food availability. Although bighorn sheep spend most of the year in alpine habitats, they usually move downslope in late winter to forage on early-season greens and then return to the high country during spring. In years of low snowfall, however, the sheep may not descend from the mountains, remaining at 10,000 to 12,000 feet. Most of the region's sizable mule deer population takes part in a lengthy, trans-Sierra migration. After wintering in sagebrush scrub east of the range, the deer cross over to the western Sierra, where they spend the summer in high-elevation meadows and riparian areas. In fall they retrace their route back

over the crest, dropping down to protected foraging areas in east side valleys and basins. Large groups of wintering deer can be seen in the vicinity of Round Valley, just northwest of Bishop.

Birds

The Eastern Sierra is home to or is visited by at least 300 species of birds. The region offers a variety of habitats for breeding, nesting, and foraging, and produces a cornucopia of foods throughout the warm-weather months. During winter, however, most of the avian population migrates to warmer climates to the south.

At least 70 bird species, however, are year-round residents. Many birds move downslope during the winter, congregating at lower elevations that provide a haven from the deep snow and cold weather of the high country. Hawks, owls, shrikes, jays, magpies, and sage grouse forage in desert scrub or pinyon-juniper woodlands. Mallards, coots, teals, and other waterfowl gather where there is open water on lakes and ponds; kingfishers and dippers fish along streams and rivers. A number of hardy species remain in the mountains all year: chickadees, nuthatches, and woodpeckers flock together in the forests, feeding on insect eggs and pupae lodged beneath the bark of conifers; Clark's nutcracker and red crossbill subsist on pine nuts and

Strutting sage grouse, Crowley Lake. FRED EBERT

buds, while blue grouse survive on a diet of pine needles. Clark's nutcracker is featured in Chapter Seven's sidebar, "Whitebark Pine and Clark's Nutcracker."

The largest number of Eastern Sierra bird species belong to a group classified as short-distance migrants. These birds arrive in late winter or spring to breed, nest, and fledge their young; they stay for the summer and like many resident species, move upslope as the season progresses. Beginning in late summer or fall they head to the southwestern U.S. and northern Mexico, dispersing to areas with mild weather and more plentiful winter food supplies. Among the short-distance migrants are many ground-foraging birds such as robins, thrashers, meadowlarks, towhees, finches, sparrows, and juncos; they are joined by a variety of waterfowl and shorebirds, including California gulls, white pelicans, plovers, grebes, sandpipers, and avocets. Mono Lake is an especially valuable habitat for migrant birds; its islands are used by 95% of the state's nesting population of California gulls, and the lake's rich invertebrate population attracts hundreds of thousands of water birds each summer.

As part of the Pacific Flyway, a broad north-south "highway" of bird migration, the Eastern Sierra is visited by many species classified as long-distance migrants. These transient species arrive in spring but soon move on, bound for breeding and nesting grounds in Alaska and Canada. They return during late summer and fall, headed toward wintering areas in Central and South America. Primarily insectivores, the long-distance migrants that visit the Eastern Sierra include many colorful species such as tanagers, orioles, grosbeaks, warblers, flycatchers, and swallows.

One of the Eastern Sierra's most celebrated long-distance migrants is the Wilson's phalarope, a handsome shorebird that journeys between Canada and South America each year. During July, over 100,000 Wilson's phalaropes create a spectacle at Mono Lake when they stop over for several weeks to rest and fatten up on brine shrimp and brine flies before continuing their journey south.

Reptiles and Amphibians
Nearly 40 species of reptiles and amphibians have been identified in the

Speckled rattlesnakes in the White Mountains, locked in a combat dance. GORDON WILTSIE

Eastern Sierra. Reptiles are common throughout the desert scrub and pinyon-juniper woodlands; near riparian areas they are joined by amphibians. Their greatest concentration and variety occurs in Owens Valley.

Temperature exercises a profound influence over the distribution and behavior of reptiles and amphibians. In the Eastern Sierra, only a few species are found above 9,000 feet, including the mountain yellow-legged frog, Yosemite toad, and Mt. Lyell salamander. As ectothermic (cold-blooded) animals, their body temperatures are primarily determined by ambient thermal conditions.

Reptiles and amphibians cannot generate significant amounts of internal body heat like mammals and birds, and they would perish in the winter conditions of the mountains. Even at lower elevations, many species withdraw from winter cold by hibernating. In summer, reptiles seek relief from the desert heat by resting in the shade and engaging in body-cooling activities such as panting.

Lizards are perhaps the most visible reptiles in the Eastern Sierra: collared lizards and chuckwallas bask on rocky slopes and lava fields; side-blotched and horned lizards dash across washes and other sandy areas; western fence lizards perch on rocks, fences, and trees. Sagebrush lizards, which are less tolerant of arid conditions than most of the area's reptiles, are absent from low-desert scrub and more common in pinyon-juniper woodlands. Gopher snakes are fairly abundant and often inhabit alluvial fans in the Owens Valley. The only venomous reptiles are the sidewinder, speckled, and western rattlesnakes; the speckled is perhaps the most widespread in the region.

Amphibians such as frogs, toads, and salamanders are not rare in the Eastern Sierra, but they are generally limited to sites near springs, creeks, ponds, and lakes; these and other aquatic habitats are essential for their survival and reproduction. The western toad and California tree frog are two of the Eastern Sierra's most widespread amphibians. By contrast, the Inyo Mountain salamander (discovered in 1973) is only found near water in its namesake range.

Fish

The Eastern Sierra's swift, tumbling creeks, clear mountain lakes, vast reservoirs, and meandering Owens River offer some of the finest angling in California. Fourteen species of fish inhabit Eastern Sierra waters, but the region is best known for its trout. East side drainages located south of Conway Summit had no trout until the 1850s, when Lahontan cutthroat trout from the East Walker River were planted in Mono Basin creeks. Golden and rainbow trout were introduced

Once widespread in Owens Valley, the Owens pupfish is now an endangered species. B. "MOOSE" PETERSON

from other parts of the Sierra Nevada during the 1870s and 1880s, and brown and eastern brook trout were released at the turn of the century. More recent introductions to the Owens River and several area reservoirs include carp, catfish, bluegill, and largemouth bass.

Four state-operated fish hatcheries in Inyo and Mono counties annually raise millions of trout that are planted in creeks and lakes throughout the Eastern Sierra. Rainbow and eastern brook trout are the two most widespread species; brown trout are common in the Owens River and larger, low-elevation bodies of water such as Crowley Lake and Bridgeport Reservoir. The brilliantly colored golden trout, California's state fish, is only found in backcountry lakes and streams. (See the sidebar in Chapter

Three, "Golden Trout.") The once-abundant Lahontan cutthroat trout has declined due to interbreeding with other trout, predation by and competition with introduced species, and habitat degradation; it is now a federally listed "threatened" species.

In addition to Lahontan cutthroat trout, four other species of fish are native to the Eastern Sierra: Owens dace, Owens sucker, Owens tui chub, and Owens pupfish. The latter two are classified as "endangered" by both federal and state wildlife agencies. Once widespread in the lower Owens River and Owens Valley ponds and wetlands, these minnow-size fish have suffered from the effects of water diversions and from predation by introduced species; today they are found in a handful of locations, most notably at Fish Slough near Bishop.

Wildflowers of the Eastern Sierra
by Mary DeDecker

The rich flora of the Eastern Sierra is worth special attention. As a result of diverse growing conditions, the region supports a wide range of plant species, some of them making handsome floral displays. A trip through Inyo and Mono counties on U.S. 395 traverses several plant communities typical of the Mojave Desert and Great Basin regions; Sierran plant communities are often nearby. A few of the most common desert species, as well as some mountain wildflowers, are described here. They may be seen along the highway, or may require an occasional side trip beyond the main route. Blooming periods are in the spring or early summer unless otherwise stated. It should be kept in mind that spring may come a month later at the most northerly sites. For those who wish to identify additional species, floral handbooks are available at museums, bookstores, and visitor centers.

The following list of wildflowers begins with species found at lower, drier sites and proceeds to those found at higher and/or wetter locations.

Desert Dandelion. *Malacothrix Californica* var. *glabrata* (Sunflower Family). This spring annual makes a sunshine-yellow border along the

Desert Dandelion. MARY DEDECKER

Bush Sunflower. MARY DEDECKER

highway or in open areas. Its 4- to 16-inch stems carry single dandelion-like flowers about one inch in diameter. The strap-shaped petals radiate from the center. Commonly found between creosote bushes in the southern Owens Valley, decreasing in abundance to the north.

Bush Sunflower, Brittlebush. *Encelia virginensis* ssp. *actonii* (Sunflower Family). Bush sunflower is a rounded shrub, mostly one to three feet high. Naked stems, each bearing a single "sunflower," rise above the leafy bush. Its gray-green leaves are triangular-ovate and about one inch long. along roadsides and in desert scrub communities.

Apricot Mallow. *Sphaeralcea ambigua* (Mallow Family). A grayish perennial, apricot mallow's leafy stems are one to three feet high. The flowers are like small hollyhocks, about one inch in diameter, and are a rich apricot color. Common and widespread in dry places, especially along roadsides.

Apricot Mallow. MARY DEDECKER

Desert Paintbrush. *Castilleja chromosa* (Snapdragon Family). A flash of bright red in the scrub communities is sure to be a clump of desert paintbrush.

Each stem is 6 to 16 inches tall and is topped with numerous red bracts. The bracts, reduced leaves that surround each flower, form a red tuft creating an impression of a paintbrush dipped in red paint. Stems are leafy with gray-green linear leaves.

Desert Paintbrush. MARY DEDECKER

Inyo Bush Lupine. *Lupinus excubitus* (Pea Family). Handsome spikes of bluish lavender, violet, or orchid flowers top the two- to four-foot-high flowering stems of this bushy perennial. Commonly found in drainage channels and on alluvial slopes.

Rabbitbrush. *Chrysothamnus nauseosus* (Sunflower Family). This relatively leafless, gray-green, two- to four-foot-high shrub is dominant where the native vegetation has been removed, such as on abandoned farmlands. The flowers are small and tubular and lack rays (daisy-like petals characteristic of many sunflower family plants), but their abundance creates a golden landscape in the fall.

Inyo Bush Lupine. MARY DEDECKER

Rabbitbrush. BILL EVARTS

Hopsage (l), and Bee Plant (r). MARY DEDECKER

Hopsage. *Grayia spinosa* (Goosefoot or Saltbush Family). Hopsage is a major component of the scrub communities in the high desert. This spiny shrub attracts attention because of its abundance of colorful seed bracts. The bracts form a sac surrounding the seed and vary in color from flesh to rose-red. The shrub, usually one to three feet high, is grayish green. Its early leaves appear frosted on the edges. Flowers are inconspicuous.

Bee Plant. *Cleome lutea* (Caper Family). Bee plant is a branching annual that grows up to four or five feet tall. Its yellow flower tufts appear at the tips of the branches. Linear, approximately one-inch-long seed pods, called "capers," are attached to slender, jointed stems. Commonly found along roadsides.

Blazing Star. DENNIS FLAHERTY

Blazing Star. *Mentzelia laevicaulis* (Loasa Family). A white-stemmed biennial, blazing star grows up to two or three feet tall. The leaves are rough to the touch and the flowers have five bright yellow petals centered around a tuft of yellow stamens. The flowers are night blooming, so the petals are closed in the morning. Common along roadsides, cut banks, or other disturbed areas.

Prickly Poppy. *Argemone munita* (Poppy Family). A very prickly perennial, prickly poppy usually grows one to three feet tall, though it can reach five feet. The large flowers have five crinkly white petals and a center of yellow stamens. Children call it the "fried egg flower." Found on dry slopes and roadsides.

Prickly Poppy. MARY DEDECKER

Desert Peach. *Prunus Andersonii* (Rose Family). A somewhat scraggly, thorny shrub, desert peach grows two to six feet high. An abundance of rose-pink blossoms appear along with the earliest small leaves (about Easter time in Mono County). Common in the sagebrush scrub community.

Desert Peach. SUE IRWIN   *Mule Ears.* GARY MOON

Mule Ears. *Wyethia mollis* (Sunflower Family). This perennial resembles a short, stout sunflower. The large, "mule-ear" leaves are ovate, somewhat woolly, and 8 to 15 inches long. Stems are one to two feet high, bearing sunflower-like blooms. Grows abundantly in slopes and swales where there is a little extra moisture.

Rose Penstemon. *Penstemon floridus* (Snapdragon Family). Rose penstemon is a perennial with one- to three-foot-tall, wandlike stems. The toothed leaves are directly opposite one another along the stem. The broad, tubular flowers are deep rose-pink and about one inch long. Found in dry, rocky places on upper alluvial fans and in lower canyons, rose penstemon is a beautiful plant, worthy of a search.

Rose Penstemon. MARY DEDECKER

Wild Iris (l). GORDON WILTSIE
Alpine Columbine (r). EDWIN ROCKWELL

Fireweed (l). DENNIS FLAHERTY
Sierra Lily (r). GORDON WILTSIE

Wild Iris. *Iris missouriensis* (Iris Family). A perennial growing from a rhizome (underground rootstock), wild iris has narrow, linear leaves. Stems are 8 to 20 inches high, bearing white to pale blue flowers. It is found in moist meadows and flats from the valley floor up to 10,000 feet. Dense populations of iris indicate over-grazing of a meadow or pasture.

Alpine Columbine. *Aquilegia pubescens* (Ranunculus Family). This perennial grows 8 to 18 inches high. Flowers are five-parted, each petal with a spur projecting backward from the base. Colors are in pastel shades, mostly pink to yellow. It is found in rocky places at high elevations. A more common columbine with red flowers, *Aquilegia formosa*, occurs along streams at lower elevations.

Shooting Star. *Dodecatheon Jeffreyi* (Primrose Family). This perennial has long, narrow leaves that grow from the base of the plant. Its naked flowering stems are usually 6 to 15 inches high. The stamens come together to form a pointed beak and the flower petals turn directly back from the stamens. The petals are magenta to lavender, rarely white. Found in wet or moist alpine meadows, shooting star often forms a field of color.

Shooting Star. GORDON WILTSIE

Sierra Lily or Small Tiger Lily. *Lilium Kelleyanum* (Lily Family). This handsome perennial grows two to four or five feet tall. Flowers are fragrant, nodding, and yellow (or yellow with some orange at the tips) with minute maroon dots. Found in wet or boggy places above 6,500 feet.

Fireweed. *Epilobium angustifolium* (Evening Primrose Family). A showy perennial growing up to several feet high, fireweed has leafy stems topped with generous clusters of flowers. Flowers are mostly lilac-purple, rarely rose or white. (A population with rose-colored flowers occurs in Onion Valley.) Commonly found in wet or moist places, often streamside, up to over 11,000 feet in the Sierra, and northward to Alaska.

Top: *Hexagonal columns of basalt at Devils Postpile.* WILLIAM NEILL
Bottom: *The fault scarp formed by the 1872 Earthquake runs north-south through the Big Pine-Taboose lava field towards Crater Mountain.* JOE POLLINI / BLM

Selected Geologic Features of the Eastern Sierra

Sites appearing in this table are listed by category as they occur from south to north.

Feature	Site	Location
FAULTS AND EARTHQUAKES		
Fault scarp	Earthquake Victims' Grave	West side of U.S. 395, just north of Lone Pine
Fault scarp	1872 Earthquake Fault	Where Mazourka Canyon Rd. dips, 3 miles east of Independence
Fault scarp (and volcanic tuff)	Fish Slough	Scarp runs along the east side of Fish Slough, about 7 miles north of Bishop
Fault scarp (and glacial moraine)	Hilton Creek Fault	National Forest campground on McGee Creek Rd., 2 miles west of U.S. 395
VOLCANISM		
Cinder cone, lava field	Red Hill and Fossil Falls	3 miles north of Little Lake, just east of U.S. 395 off Cinder Rd.
Lava field, cinder cones	Big Pine-Taboose Lava Field	15 miles north of Independence on both sides of valley near the junction of U.S. 395 and Taboose Creek Rd.
Volcanic ash and tuff	Volcanic Tableland	Summit of Sherwin Grade on U.S. 395 and Owens River Gorge area to the east
Hot springs	Hot Creek Geologic Site	Follow signs from U.S. 395 to Fish Hatchery and continue 2.5 miles
Dormant volcano	Mammoth Mountain	Take Mammoth Mountain Ski Area gondola to the summit
Columnar basalt	Devils Postpile	Devils Postpile National Monument
Volcanic crater/ explosion pit	Inyo Craters	Take signed dirt road north from Mammoth Scenic Loop; short hike to the craters
Lava dome	Obsidian Dome	Take Glass Flow Rd. west from U.S. 395 at Deadman Summit
Lava dome	Panum Crater	Off north side of Highway 120, about 3 miles east of U.S. 395; short hike to the crater summit
Dormant volcano	Negit Island	In Mono Lake

Feature	Site	Location
GLACIATION		
Glacier (vista)	**Palisade Glacier**	Best seen from Highway 168, just east of Big Pine
Glacial moraine, glacier (vista)	**Big Pine Canyon**	Moraines along Big Pine Canyon Rd., vista from roadend near Glacier Lodge
Glacial moraine (vista)	**Pine Creek Canyon**	Look south to mouth of Pine Creek Canyon from U.S. 395 Scenic Point turnout on Sherwin Grade, 12 miles north of Bishop
Glacial moraine	**Convict Lake**	Convict Lake Rd., approaching lake
Glacial polish	**Devils Postpile**	Top of basalt columns at Devils Postpile
Glacial moraine	**Lee Vining Canyon**	Along Highway 120, just west of Lee Vining
Glacial moraine	**Twin Lakes**	Approaching Twin Lakes from Bridgeport
WEATHERING AND EROSION		
Sand dunes	**Olancha Dunes**	Take Highway 190 about 4 miles east from Olancha, turn south on dirt road
Weathered granite	**Alabama Hills**	Take Whitney Portal Rd. 2.8 miles west of Lone Pine, turn north on Movie Rd.
Alluvial fans	**White-Inyo Range and Sierra Nevada**	Good examples: east of Big Pine, drive up alluvial fan on Highway 168; also, base of Mt. Tom west of Bishop
ANCIENT LAKES AND RIVERS		
Ancient riverbed	**Fossil Falls**	3 miles north of Little Lake, take Cinder Rd. east from U.S. 395; short hike to the "falls"
Ancient lake shore(s) (vista)	**Owens Lake**	Ancient shorelines visible from Horseshoe Meadow Rd., 7 to 20 miles from Lone Pine
Tufa towers	**Mono Lake**	South Tufa Area on Mono Lake or County Park on north side of lake
Ancient lake shore terraces, tufa	**Mono Lake**	Highway 167, 1.3 miles east of U.S. 395 on north side of Mono Lake

Lateral moraines mark a glacier's path along Green Creek near Bridgeport. JOHN S. SHELTON

Major Plant Communities of the Eastern Sierra

Plant Community	Distribution/Elevation	Characteristic Species	Sample Locations
WETLAND			
Riparian Wetland	Owens Valley, Long Valley, Mono Basin, Sierra Nevada, and White-Inyo Range from 3,000 to 10,500 feet	Willow, cottonwood, water birch, quaking aspen, sedge, rush, streamside paintbrush, monkshood, goldenrod, columbine (species vary with site and elevation)	Owens River, Independence Creek (Onion Valley), Big Pine Creek, Bishop Creek, Fish Slough, Rock Creek, Lee Vining Creek, Mill Creek (Lundy Canyon), Green Creek
Alkali Sink Wetland	Lower Owens Valley around Owens Lake and occasional sites on the valley floor from 3,600 to 3,800 feet	Salt grass, alkali weed, ink weed, alkali bird's beak, Parry's salt bush, naked cleome, wild heliotrope	Swansea, Dirty Socks Springs, Cottonwood Charcoal Kilns
SCRUB			
Sand Dune Scrub	Owens Valley, Mono Basin from 3,600 to 6,600 feet	Greasewood, Kearny's buckwheat, naked cleome, Nuttall's tiquilia, milk vetch, northern sand verbena, rice grass	South and east shores of Owens Lake; north and east shores of Mono Lake
Greasewood Scrub	Lower Owens Valley, Inyo Mountains from 3,600 to 4,000 feet	Greasewood, shadscale, alkali sacaton, iodine bush or pickle bush, broom aster	Lower Owens River via Manzanar-Reward Rd. or Mazourka Canyon Rd., Highway 168 east of Big Pine
Creosote Bush Scrub	Owens Valley, Sierra Nevada to 3,600 feet; White-Inyo Range from 4,000 to 5,000 feet	Creosote bush, burro bush, cheese bush, brittle bush, blister dalea or indigo bush, inflated buckwheat, apricot mallow, beavertail cactus, Joshua tree (S. Owens Valley)	Fossil Falls, Owens Lake area (outer perimeter), east side of Owens Valley up into Mazourka Canyon
Shadscale Scrub	Owens Valley, Sierra Nevada from 3,600 to 4,000 feet; White-Inyo Range from 3,600 to 6,500 feet	Shadscale, spiny mendora, spiny hopsage, lamb's tail or winterfat, bud sage, blackbrush, cheese bush, apricot mallow, blister dalea or indigo bush, beavertail cactus, desert allysum, saucer plant, golden bush, rabbitbrush, birdnest buckwheat, Nevada ephedra	Alabama Hills, Manzanar, lower Mazourka Canyon, base of Westgard Pass, Bridgeport Valley
Sagebrush Scrub	Long Valley, Mono Basin, Bridgeport Valley, Sierra Sierra Nevada from 4,000 to 7,500 feet	Great Basin sagebrush, rabbitbrush, antelope and desert bitterbrush, low sagebrush, Adonis or Inyo bush lupine, desert peach, California or bee buckwheat, Nevada ephedra, cottonthorn	Crowley Lake, Mono Lake area, upper Owens River, any road along the east base of the Sierra Nevada
Great Basin Montane Scrub	White-Inyo Range from 8,500 to 10,500 feet	Low sagebrush, mountain mahogany, wax currant, Great Basin sagebrush, alpine sagebrush, fern bush or desert sweet, mock orange, cream bush, showy penstemon, curl-leaf rabbitbrush, snowberry, blue elderberry, desert figwort	White Mountain Road above Sierra View Overlook

DESERT WOODLAND

Pinyon-Juniper Woodland	Mono Basin, Sierra Nevada from 6,500 to 7,500 feet; White-Inyo Range from 6,500 to 9,000 feet	Pinyon pine, Utah juniper, black sagebrush or broom sagebrush, desert bitterbrush, desert snowberry, newberry milk vetch, Inyo milk vetch, purple bird's beak or Heller bird's beak, green ephedra, Inyo Mountain penstemon	Lower Whitney Portal Road, lower Onion Valley Road, Cerro Gordo, upper Mazourka Canyon, Badger Flat, Westgard Pass, Volcanic Tableland, Sherwin Grade (U.S. 395), Bodie Hills

CONIFEROUS FOREST

Jeffrey Pine Forest	Mono Basin, Sierra Nevada from 7,500 to 8,500 feet	Jeffrey pine, white fir, quaking aspen, Great Basin sagebrush, mountain mahogany, antelope bitterbrush, Parry's rabbitbrush, mule ears, mountain pennyroyal, white-veined wintergreen	Whitney Portal, Big Pine Canyon, Bishop Creek, Inyo Craters, Lookout Mountain, June Lake, Mono Mills, Twin Lakes
Red Fir Forest	Sierra Nevada from 8,000 to 9,000 feet	Red fir, wintergreen (Mature red fir forest sometimes includes bush chinquapin, snowberry, gooseberry, manzanita, and lodgepole pine.)	Devils Postpile, west of Inyo Craters, Highway 203 between Mammoth Lakes and Mammoth Mountain Ski Area
Lodgepole Pine Forest	Sierra Nevada from 8,000 to 9,500 feet	Lodgepole pine, red fir, quaking aspen, mountain heather, Brewer's cinquefoil, fireweed	Upper Rock Creek Canyon, Mammoth Lakes Basin, Virginia Lakes
Subalpine Coniferous Forest	Sierra Nevada from 8,500 to 11,500 feet	Whitebark pine, lodgepole pine, foxtail pine, limber pine, quaking aspen, gooseberry, alpine sagebrush, oval-leaved buckwheat, harlequin buckwheat, cinquefoil, Sierra Nevada primrose	Horseshoe Meadow, Minaret Summit, Tioga Pass, upper Virginia Lakes
Western Bristlecone Pine Forest	White-Inyo Range from 9,500 to 11,500 feet	Limber pine, western bristlecone pine, wax currant, golden bush, mountain mahogany, rabbitbrush, alpine sagebrush, low sagebrush, alpine paintbrush, fern bush, cushion phlox, White Mountain or raspberry buckwheat, oval-leaved buckwheat, limestone aster, prickly milk vetch	Schulman Grove, Patriarch Grove

ALPINE FELL-FIELDS

Sierra Nevada Alpine Fell-fields	Sierra Nevada above 11,000 feet	Alpine willow, alpine laurel, alpine columbine, rock fringe, mountain sorrel, sky pilot, Davidson's penstemon, Sierra Nevada primrose, alpine paintbrush, alpine gold	Mount Whitney, Kearsarge Pass
White Mountains Alpine Fell-fields	White-Inyo Range above 11,500 feet	Yellow cushion cress, Mono clover, snow buckwheat, White Mountain or raspberry buckwheat, alpine bluegrass, pygmy daisy, heterodox or whorlflower penstemon, cinquefoil, pygmy bitterroot, White Mountain sky pilot, alpine gold	White Mountain Road above Patriarch Grove

Common Mammals and Birds of the Eastern Sierra

The species in this table are grouped into general Eastern Sierra habitats where they are most characteristic or visible. Although each species appears in only one category, many also occur in adjoining habitats. Especially widespread species are followed by an asterisk (*). For transient or hard-to-see species, the following abbreviations indicate the season in which they are most visible or audible: (Sp) = spring, (Su) = summer, (F) = fall, (W) = winter. A species associated with riparian areas is followed by an (R).

Habitat	Selected Viewing Areas
Lakes, Reservoirs, Ponds, and Wetlands **Widespread Viewing** Birds: American avocet (Sp-F), bald eagle (W), common snipe, California gull* (Sp-F), Canada goose, cinnamon teal (Sp, Su), eared grebe, great blue heron, green-winged teal (F-Sp), mallard, red-necked phalarope (Su), red-winged blackbird, osprey (Su, W), Wilson's phalarope (Su), white pelican (Sp-F), yellow-headed blackbird (Sp, Su)	Tinemaha Reservoir, Crowley Lake, June Lake, Mono Lake, Bridgeport Reservoir
Limited Viewing Snowy plover (Su) Tundra (whistling) swan (W)	Mono Lake Tinemaha Reservoir
Low-Desert Scrub and Valley Floors **Widespread Viewing** Mammals: coyote,* Audubon's cottontail, little pocket mouse, Merriam's kangaroo rat, white-tailed antelope ground squirrel Birds: black-billed magpie, black-throated sparrow, horned lark,* kestrel,* loggerhead shrike, mourning dove, roadrunner, red-tailed hawk,* Say's phoebe, valley quail, western meadowlark, common raven*	Fossil Falls, Owens Lake, Alabama Hills, lower Mazourka Canyon, Lone Pine, Independence, Bishop, Fish Slough, Mono Basin
Limited Viewing Tule elk	Near Owens River, Bishop to Owens Lake delta
High-Desert Scrub and Pinyon-Juniper Woodland **Widespread Viewing** Mammals: black-tailed jackrabbit,* California ground squirrel, desert woodrat, least chipmunk, Nuttall's cottontail, mule deer* (W), Panamint chipmunk, Panamint kangaroo rat, pinyon mouse Birds: blue-gray gnatcatcher, Brewer's sparrow, green-tailed towhee, pinyon jay, sage sparrow, sage thrasher	Volcanic Tableland, Lower Rock Creek, Long Valley, Mono Basin, Bridgeport Valley, upper Mazourka Canyon, lower White Mountain Rd.
Limited Viewing Pronghorn (Su) Sage grouse (most visible in late Feb and early March)	Bodie Hills, Hammil Valley Long Valley, Bodie Hills

Lower- and Middle-Elevation Forests and Meadows

Widespread Viewing

Mammals: beaver* (R), black bear, bobcat, deer mouse,* golden-mantled ground squirrel, bushy-tailed woodrat, Douglas squirrel (or chickaree), pine marten, striped skunk, lodgepole chipmunk, porcupine

Birds: dipper or water ouzel (R), American robin,* belted kingfisher (R), Cassin's finch (Su), northern flicker,* Oregon dark-eyed junco,* red-breasted sapsucker (R), Steller's jay,* violet-green swallow (Sp, Su), western tanager (Su), western wood pewee (Su)

Whitney Portal, Big Pine Canyon, Bishop Creek Canyon, Rock Creek Canyon, Mammoth Lakes Basin, Devils Postpile, Inyo Craters, June Lake, Lee Vining Canyon, Lundy Canyon, Twin Lakes

High-Elevation Forests and Meadows

Widespread Viewing

Mammals: alpine chipmunk, Belding ground squirrel,* pika, white-tailed jackrabbit, yellow-bellied marmot

Birds: blue grouse, Clark's nutcracker,* golden eagle,* mountain bluebird (Su), mountain chickadee,* rosy finch, white-crowned sparrow,* yellow-rumped warbler

Horseshoe Meadow, Onion Valley, upper Rock Creek, Minaret Summit, Tioga Pass area, Virginia Lakes, Schulman Grove (not all species)

Limited Viewing

Bighorn sheep

Baxter Pass area (west of Independence), Lee Vining Canyon, Sawmill Canyon in winter

Average Temperatures and Annual Precipitation in the Eastern Sierra						
Weather Station	Average Annual Precipitation	Average Daily High and Low Temperatures in Degrees Fahrenheit for Selected Months				
	Total Inches	January	April	July	October	
Independence El. 3,925 ft.	5.6 inches	Hi: 54 Lo: 28	Hi: 72 Lo: 42	Hi: 97 Lo: 64	Hi: 79 Lo: 45	
Bishop El. 4,110 ft.	5.6 inches	Hi: 53 Lo: 21	Hi: 72 Lo: 36	Hi: 97 Lo: 55	Hi: 76 Lo: 37	
Crowley Lake El. 6,781 ft.	10.2 inches	n/a	n/a	n/a	n/a	
Mammoth Lakes El. 7,800 ft.	23.0 inches*	Hi: 37 Lo: n/a	Hi: 54 Lo: n/a	Hi: 79 Lo: n/a	Hi: 65 Lo: n/a	
Mono Lake El. 6,375 ft.	14.0 inches	Hi: 40 Lo: 19	Hi: 58 Lo: 29	Hi: 84 Lo: 49	Hi: 65 Lo: 34	
Bridgeport El. 6,465 ft.	10.1 inches	Hi: 43 Lo: 9	Hi: 58 Lo: 21	Hi: 83 Lo: 39	Hi: 67 Lo: 22	
Crooked Creek Laboratory (White Mountains) El. 10,500 ft.	13.8 inches	Hi: 30 Lo: 9	Hi: 40 Lo: 19	Hi: 65 Lo: 40	Hi: 50 Lo: 26	
Barcroft Laboratory (White Mountains) El. 12,500 ft.	19.3 inches	Hi: 23 Lo: 8	Hi: 28 Lo: 12	Hi: 54 Lo: 37	Hi: 40 Lo: 24	

* Precipitation totals vary considerably in this area; precipitation is much higher to the west of Mammoth Lakes.

History of the Eastern Sierra

T he nature of a land determines in some wise the manner of the life there. This is a large country, with few and far-between oases of richness and greenness. One may take days' journeys in it and not come by any place or occasion whereby men might live; and other days stumble upon the wealth of dreams. Weeks on end the traveler finds no towns nor places where towns could be, and then drops suddenly into close hives of men, digging, jostling, fighting, drinking, lusting and rejoicing. Every story of that country is colored by the fashion of the life there; breaking up in swift, passionate intervals between long, dun stretches, like the land that out of hot sinks of desolation heaves up great bulks of granite ranges with opal shadows playing in their shining, snow-piled curves.

—Mary Austin,

"The Lost Mine of Fisherman's Peak," 1903

Left: The Carson & Colorado's Engine #18 in Independence. BILL EVARTS
Opposite: Bodie, the largest unrestored ghost town in the West. LEWIS KEMPER

The "Slim Princess" served Owens Valley until 1960. EASTERN CALIFORNIA MUSEUM

A Tumultuous History

Flanked on the west by the towering Sierra Nevada and insulated on the north, south, and east by vast deserts, the Eastern Sierra remained one of the last regions of California to be explored and settled by whites. Semi-nomadic Paiute and Shoshone Indians inhabited the territory east of the Sierra when the first whites—small parties of fur trappers and explorers—traveled through the area during the 1830s and 1840s. The Indians'

traditional way of life came to an end during the 1860s as miners and pioneers poured into the region in search of gold and arable land.

Governed by the sudden rise and fall of local mining operations, the Eastern Sierra economy grew rapidly from the 1860s through the 1880s. Two of California's richest mineral lodes—Cerro Gordo (silver) and Bodie (gold)—were discovered during this period. Mining activity waned toward the end of the 19th century, but ranching and farming, especially in the water-rich Owens Valley, injected new-found prosperity and stability the region's economy.

Shortly after the turn of the century, the fast-growing city of Los Angeles became interested in the bountiful waters of the Eastern Sierra. Los Angeles touched off a decades-long "water war" when it surreptitiously purchased key land and water rights along the Owens River and then built an aqueduct to deliver the water to Los Angeles-area homes and farms. By the late 1920s, Los Angeles controlled most of the Eastern Sierra's water rights, and the once-prosperous farming area of Owens Valley had plunged into recession.

The most recent phase of growth in the Eastern Sierra began in the 1940s and 1950s as Californians began to vacation in the region, revitalizing its economy with their tourist dollars. They had discovered the Eastern Sierra's greatest resources—clean air, open space, stunning scenery, and unparalleled year-round recreation.

Early Exploration of the Eastern Sierra

Although 17th-century Spanish maps of *Alta California* showed *las Sierras Nevadas*, or "snowy ranges," the great mountain range that now bears the name Sierra Nevada was probably not seen by whites until the 18th century. Spaniards Fray Juan Crespi and Pedro Fages wrote the first descriptions of the Sierra after viewing the range from the San Joaquin Valley in 1772. The following century, a 27-year-old American fur trapper named Jedediah Smith became the first white man to cross the Sierra Nevada. Smith led a small band of trappers to southern California by way of the Mojave Desert in 1826. Returning to United States territory the next year, Smith made his historic crossing of the Sierra—from west to east—cresting the range near Ebbetts Pass north of Yosemite.

In the summer of 1833, U.S. Army Captain B. L. E. Bonneville dispatched 70 men to explore the territory from the Great Salt Lake west to California. Commanded by Bonneville's trusted lieutenant, Joseph Reddeford Walker, the detachment crossed present-day Nevada and entered the Sierra west of Bridgeport Valley. Despite early snows, the expedition struggled over the mountains in the fall of 1833, achieving the first east-to-west crossing of the range by white explorers. In the spring of 1834, Walker left the San Joaquin Valley and followed an Indian trail up the Kern River drainage. He then skirted the south end of the Sierra on the route known today as Walker Pass. Walker traveled north through Owens Valley to rejoin his westward trail, becoming the first white man to travel along the Sierra's eastern escarpment.

Walker retraced his steps along this Owens Valley/Walker Pass route while guiding emigrants—the Chiles party—to the San Joaquin Valley in 1843. Two years later, Walker joined an expedition led by Captain John Charles Frémont, who had been commissioned to find overland routes to California. While Frémont crossed the Sierra near Lake Tahoe with a handful of men, Walker led most of the party south through Owens Valley and over Walker Pass to eventually rejoin Frémont in the San Joaquin Valley. Richard Owens, a close friend of Frémont, crossed the Sierra with Frémont's group and never saw the valley and river that the expedition leader later named for him.

Scattered adventurers may have made their way along the Sierra's east side from time to time, but the next documented account concerns the 1852 expedition of Lieutenant Tredwell Moore. An army officer stationed at Fort Miller, near present-day Fresno, Lt. Moore was dispatched to punish Yosemite Miwok Indians for the alleged murder of three white prospectors. Most of the Miwoks, led by Chief Teneiya, fled to safety in the Mono Basin, but Moore's forces captured and executed six Miwok men in the Yosemite high country. The group then crossed the Sierra to Mono Lake, following a well-established Indian trading route, the Mono Trail. Failing to locate Chief Teneiya, Lt. Moore returned to the San Joaquin Valley, carrying samples of gold-bearing quartz from the Mono Lake region.

Moore's expedition was to have lasting consequences. In the fall of 1852, not long after Lt. Moore's return, Leroy Vining and several partners headed across the range in search of gold. Vining stayed on to become the first white settler in the Eastern Sierra and spent several years prospecting near Mono Basin and Tioga Pass. Although he never discovered gold or silver, Vining prospered from his sawmill in Lee Vining Canyon which supplied lumber and firewood to incoming prospectors during the region's mining boom in the early 1860s.

From 1855 to 1857, Alexis W. von Schmidt directed California's first official surveys of Mono Basin and Owens Valley. His mapping was

Top: California's State Geological Survey field party of 1864. From left: Gardner, Cotter, Brewer, and King. Courtesy of BANCROFT LIBRARY
Bottom: Old ranch house and corral near Bishop. BILL EVARTS

Above: Petroglyphs in the Volcanic Tableland north of Bishop. BILL EVARTS
Opposite: Edna Power and baby Hazel Richards, Owens Valley Paiutes, 1912. EASTERN CALIFORNIA MUSEUM / A.A. FORBES

remarkably accurate, and his journals were later studied for their detailed observations of Owens Valley Paiutes. The Eastern Sierra was further mapped in 1864, when William Brewer led California's first geological survey of the southeastern Sierra Nevada. His party identified and named some of the Sierra's tallest peaks, including Mount Whitney. During the late 19th century, mountaineers such as Clarence King and John Muir explored the remote high country of the Sierra Nevada and helped open the way to recreation in the range Muir called "the most divinely beautiful of all the mountain chains."

Native Americans in the Eastern Sierra

Paiute and Shoshone people have lived in the Eastern Sierra for at least 1,000 years. They were preceded by other Native American groups; spearheads that are over 10,000 years old have been discovered in the Eastern Sierra. Other artifacts found in the region can be traced to the Pinto Basin Indians who migrated from southeastern California to the northern end of the White Mountains about 5,000 years ago. Indian petroglyphs (prehistoric rock carvings) are etched into boulders at a number of Owens Valley locations, intriguing and mysterious remnants of previous

cultures. This native "rock art" may never be completely understood by anthropologists, since even 19th-century Paiutes claimed ignorance of its meaning.

While Shoshones inhabited southern Owens Valley and desert lands farther east, Paiutes ranged throughout Owens Valley, Mono Basin, Bridgeport Valley, and north into Oregon. Known to themselves as "Numu"—the people—the Paiutes spent most of their time in subsistence-related activities. White explorers and settlers originated the word Paiute, a name they applied to Native Americans throughout the Great Basin.

For the Paiutes, life was centered around the family group, but clans joined for yearly celebrations. They often crossed the Sierra to trade and socialize with the Miwok and Yokut people who lived on the western side of the range.

Most Paiutes and Shoshones were migratory, moving several times a year to take advantage of seasonally available food. They fished, hunted a variety of game, harvested seeds from several species of bunch grass, dug bulbs and tubers, and collected nuts, berries, and fruits. Pinyon pine nuts were the principal source of winter sustenance. Among the Paiutes' foods were two types of insects: the caterpillars of the Pandora moth, gathered in Jeffrey pine forests, and the pupae of the brine (or alkali) fly, collected from the shores of Owens and Mono lakes. In Owens Valley, the Paiutes also devised a system of watering fields of taboose (*Cyperus esculentus*), a wild plant that produces a small, edible tuber.

During the 1860s and 1870s, the influx of pioneers—and the tens of thousands of cattle and sheep that were driven into the Eastern Sierra valleys—had a devastating impact on the Paiutes' food resources. Large areas of pinyon and Jeffrey pine were clear-cut for lumber, fuel, and mine-shaft timbers; livestock trampled and grazed meadows that provided edible roots, tubers, and seeds; game and waterfowl populations were decimated by relentless hunting.

Tension between the Indians and encroaching settlers was most acute in Owens Valley, where desperate Paiutes occasionally resorted to cattle rustling for food. Despite peace-making efforts by both white and Paiute leaders, confrontations between the Indians and pioneers led to violence and bloodshed. Besieged by settlers' requests for military assistance, the United States government sent a detachment of about 200 soldiers from Fort Latham (near Los Angeles) to Owens Valley. Led by Colonel George S. Evans, the troops established Camp Independence on July 4, 1862.

A peace treaty was signed in October 1862. The Paiutes were plied

with gifts and provisions, and an Owens Valley Indian reservation was proposed by southern California's Superintendent of Indian Affairs. Several months of uneasy peace followed, but fighting renewed in March 1863. U.S. troops from central California and western Nevada converged on Owens Valley, engaging the Indians in several decisive battles. By late spring, the Paiutes had been defeated and many of their food caches destroyed; in June, hundreds arrived at Camp Independence to surrender. The garrison was closed in July, and about 900 Paiutes—most of the valley's Indian population—were marched in the heat of summer from Independence to the San Sebastian

Reservation near Fort Tejon.

The Indian wars briefly flared up again in December 1864 after Paiutes murdered two pioneers in southern Owens Valley. Settlers retaliated by killing 35 Indians who were camped near the shore of Owens Lake. This massacre prompted the return of troops to Camp Independence, and within two years reports of violent confrontations between Indians and whites had ceased. By the end of the decade many Paiutes had returned to Owens Valley, seeking work as laborers on farms and ranches that now occupied their ancestral lands.

Gold and Silver Mining Heyday: 1857 to 1887

The Eastern Sierra's mining heyday began with the discovery of gold placers near Bridgeport Valley in 1857. This modest strike, at a site the miners named Dogtown, touched off the first gold rush to the east side of the range. The following year, rich ledges of gold were uncovered at Monoville, a few miles south of Dogtown. By 1859, hundreds of miners had made their way over the Sierra to work the promising diggings at Monoville. The mining excitement generated by Dogtown and Monoville was overshadowed by the big silver strike at nearby Esmeralda (Aurora), Nevada. Mining fever soon gripped the entire east side of the Sierra, and by 1860 claims were being worked from Virginia City, Nevada to the Coso Range southeast of Owens Lake.

During the 1860s, mining camps sprang up in the mountains on both sides of Owens Valley. The 1865 discovery of silver near the crest of the Inyo Mountains above Owens Lake triggered nearly two decades of development in the Eastern Sierra. Named *Cerro Gordo*, Spanish for "Fat Hill," the site became the richest silver-mining district in California history. Anticipating further mining activity in Inyo County, owners of the Carson & Colorado Railroad extended the line from western Nevada to southern Owens Valley in 1883. Forging a link that joined Eastern Sierra towns to transcontinental rail lines near Carson City, Nevada, the railroad helped bring an end to the region's isolation.

The richest gold deposits in the Eastern Sierra were found in the windswept Bodie Hills northeast of Mono Lake. Gold placers were first discovered there in 1859 by Monoville prospector William Bodey. The site yielded little mineral wealth until 1877, when the newly established Standard Mine Company began extracting gold ore from a rich vein. Word of the company's success spread quickly, and almost overnight Bodie's population mushroomed to 6,000. Bodie earned a reputation as one of the most violent and lawless mining camps in the West, but by 1888 the mines of the Bodie Hills were depleted, and only a handful of residents inhabited the once-notorious mining camp.

Mining operations spawned boomtowns in other parts of the Eastern Sierra during the late 1870s. Two of the largest camps were Lundy, west of Mono Lake, and Mammoth City, near the Mammoth Lakes Basin. But most Eastern Sierra mining ventures faded by the mid-1880s, and ranching and farming emerged as the driving force in the region's economy. The mines of Cerro Gordo and Bodie were reworked in the early 20th century, but mining never regained a dominant role in Eastern Sierra life.

The Growth of Ranching and Farming

The region's flurry of mining activity provided a tremendous stimulus to ranching, farming, logging, and road-building. Mining camps were ready-made markets for the surplus produce and livestock raised on homesteads in areas such as the Bridgeport Valley, Mono Basin, and Owens Valley. The demand for lumber and firewood—especially at Cerro Gordo and Bodie—was almost insatiable. During the 1860s and 1870s, sawmills were established in wooded canyons along the east side of the Sierra, and by the 1880s, commercial lumbering was

Workers at the Reward Mine in the Inyo Mountains, late 1800s. EASTERN CALIFORNIA MUSEUM

Main Street in Bishop, 1886. EASTERN CALIFORNIA MUSEUM / C.E. PETERSON

underway in the forests south of Mono Lake. The logistical support required by the mines spurred the building of new roads throughout the region, including the Sonora and Mono Road (Sonora Pass), the Great Sierra Wagon Road (Tioga Pass), and the first road up Sherwin Grade, between Bishop and Mammoth, a precursor to U.S. 395.

Bridgeport was one of the first local settlements outside the mining camps. Strategically located between the eastern Sierra Nevada and mining districts in western Nevada, Bridgeport became the seat of government for California's newly formed Mono County in 1864. Bridgeport Valley ranchers and merchants prospered during the gold rush to Bodie, when thousands of newcomers flocked to the Sierra's east side. Settlers in Mono Basin also benefited from the rapid growth of Bodie, providing the miners

with produce, livestock, lumber, and firewood. The basin's pioneers even marketed gull eggs, collected from nesting grounds on the islands of Mono Lake. Following the decline of Bodie's mines, ranching became the mainstay of Mono County's economy. By the turn of the century, small resorts were catering to summer visitors at Mammoth and Mono Lake—harbingers of the modern tourist industry that blossomed decades later.

The abundance of forage and water in Owens Valley attracted many of its first immigrants. Fleeing drought-parched grazing lands, San Joaquin Valley ranchers drove thousands of cattle and sheep over Walker Pass and into the meadows of Owens Valley in 1861. Among these ranchers were Samuel Bishop and his wife, who brought 500 head of cattle to upper Owens Valley and established a camp

near the present site of Bishop. Owens Valley settlement was further stimulated by the discovery of gold and silver in both the Sierra Nevada and White-Inyo Range. Inyo County was formed in 1866, and Independence, site of the valley's first pioneer homestead, was voted its seat of government.

Owens Valley farmers and ranchers prospered as the population of nearby mining camps swelled during the 1870s. Although mining activity waned during the 1880s and 1890s, the valley's agricultural economy continued to grow. It was dominated by sheep and cattle ranching, and to a lesser extent, the production of crops such as apples, grapes, alfalfa, potatoes, wheat, corn, and honey. By 1903, Owens Valley was home to several thousand people, it had its own bank, electric plant, public high school, and the region's only incorporated city—Bishop.

The Owens Valley Water War

Soon after the turn of the century, Owens Valley citizens became embroiled with the City of Los Angeles in a bitter struggle over future rights to the Owens River and its tributaries. The Eastern Sierra water controversy began in 1903, when the newly created U.S. Reclamation Service sent a team of engineers to study the feasibility of launching a federal

Hauling aqueduct pipe with 52-mule team. EASTERN CALIFORNIA MUSEUM / CITY OF LOS ANGELES

irrigation project in Owens Valley. They reported that the Owens River was underutilized, and that by damming the river above Bishop in Long Valley, Owens Valley farmers would have enough water to irrigate at least 60,000 additional acres.

Among those most interested in the Owens Valley survey was Fred Eaton, the former mayor of Los Angeles. Eaton's good friend, Joseph Lippincott, was the regional engineer for the Reclamation Service. Lippincott was directed to head up the federal government's Owens River Project, and he hired Eaton to serve as his "consultant." Los Angeles boosters like Eaton and Lippincott were acutely aware that the future growth of their city would require a bountiful supply of imported water—and the Owens River drainage looked like the best place to get it. In 1904, Eaton, Lippincott, and Los Angeles water superintendent William Mulholland secretly laid plans for one of the greatest water grabs in U.S. history.

Representing himself as an agent of the Reclamation Service, Fred Eaton made generous offers for Owens Valley land and water rights; Owens Valley citizens, anticipating the rewards of the proposed reclamation project, were eager to cooperate by selling portions of their land. Using his own money (he was later repaid by the city), Eaton purchased key properties for an aqueduct project and transferred the titles to Los Angeles. Lippincott quietly lobbied the Reclamation Service to shelve its Owens Valley project. Mulholland visited the Eastern Sierra to reconnoiter the water situation and mapped out his ambitious plan for an aqueduct that would carry Owens River water over 200 miles across the desert to Los Angeles. In July 1905, the *Los Angeles Times* jubilantly broke the news about the aqueduct with a headline that trumpeted "Titanic Project to Give the City a River."

Owens Valley citizens were stunned, but many became resigned to the idea of exporting valley water for domestic use in urban Los Angeles. They were outraged, though, at the prospect of providing surplus water— at the expense of local farms and ranches—to irrigate crops in the dry San Fernando Valley on the outskirts of Los Angeles. The city's leaders, however, were determined to lock up a future water supply for the fast-growing metropolis, even if it meant that most of the water would initially flow into San Fernando Valley irrigation ditches.

Owens Valley residents failed to persuade the Reclamation Service and

President Theodore Roosevelt to keep the reclamation project alive. By June 1906, when the aqueduct issue was put to a vote in the U.S. Congress, Los Angeles representatives had convinced the lawmakers to strip an amendment from the legislation that would have guaranteed irrigation rights to Owens Valley farmers. The valley's fate was further sealed when tens of thousands of acres of public land—sagebrush-covered acreage that would have been part of the federal reclamation project—were added to the new Inyo National Forest and made off-limits to homesteading.

When aqueduct construction began in 1907, "double agent" Lippincott resigned his job with the Reclamation Service and began working as William Mulholland's deputy at the Los Angeles Department of Water and Power. The 233-mile aqueduct, relying solely on gravity to transport the water, ranks among the most impressive engineering feats in United States history. It is a credit to William Mulholland that the project was completed on schedule and within budget; from 1907 to its completion in 1913, the aqueduct was built amid a storm of controversy, including allegations of an insiders' real estate scheme in San Fernando Valley, a labor strike, opposition by private utility companies, and continued pressure from Owens Valley citizens. Charges were even made that a

drought had been fabricated to persuade Los Angeles voters to approve the project's hefty $23 million water bond.

Despite the construction of the aqueduct and the abandonment of the reclamation project, farmers in the Big Pine and Bishop areas—above the aqueduct's intake—had ample water. But during the early 1920s California experienced a series of dry years, and in 1923, as water volume in the Los Angeles aqueduct steadily dwindled, the city launched an aggressive campaign of land purchases to consolidate its control of the river's upstream waters. Within a few years Los Angeles had secured water rights to most of the major irrigation canals in the upper Owens Valley.

Faced with the demise of their irrigation-based economy, many Owens Valley citizens began pushing for what seemed to be their only option—a complete purchase of Owens Valley by Los Angeles and payment of reparations to failing businesses and farms. The refusal of Los Angeles to admit responsibility for the area's economic troubles was regarded with disbelief, and it fostered a growing militancy among valley leaders. In November 1924, Owens Valley citizens took control of the Alabama Gates (aqueduct floodgates) north of Lone Pine. During their five-day occupation, aqueduct water was diverted back into the Owens River

channel, and the Eastern Sierra water controversy received worldwide publicity. Owens Valley unity was at its height as a hundred or more families gathered at the site for picnics and visiting. The peaceful siege ended when Los Angeles officials consented to pursue an agreement with Owens Valley irrigators.

By 1927 no accord had been reached and Owens Valley residents launched a state-wide brochure campaign to publicize their plight. That same year, a series of dynamite blasts wreaked havoc on the aqueduct. Los Angeles dispatched a trainload of detectives armed with machine guns and rifles; roadblocks were thrown up and searchlights probed the valley.

Ironically, the citizens of Owens Valley were soon defeated from within. The Watterson brothers,

U.S. 395 crosses the aqueduct a few miles north of Lone Pine. BILL EVARTS

owners of the Inyo County Bank and prominent leaders in the fight for local water rights, were convicted of embezzlement and sent to prison in November 1927. The collapse of the Watterson's five banks, which held the mortgages to many local farms, sent Owens Valley spiraling into recession. The following year, Los Angeles purchased more property along the Owens River and its tributaries. During the Depression years many Owens Valley families moved away, and the population of Owens Valley declined.

Los Angeles purchased additional land and water rights along streams in the Mammoth area and in Mono Basin during the 1930s. In 1941, the Long Valley Dam was built at the head of the Owens River Gorge to impound Crowley Lake Reservoir. That same year, the aqueduct was extended north to Mono Basin to collect water diverted from four more mountain streams. The next stage of the water project was completed three decades later; in 1970 Los Angeles constructed a second aqueduct to handle increased surface water exports from Mono Basin and groundwater pumped from city-owned wells in Owens Valley.

The export of Eastern Sierra water continues to generate controversy, litigation, and legislative attempts at compromise. The key issues being contested are water diversions from Mono Basin and groundwater pumping in Owens Valley. As a result of Mono Basin water diversions, Mono Lake has become increasingly saline. If the lake becomes too salty, many biologists fear that its unique ecosystem, which serves as an important stopover and feeding area for millions of migrating birds, could collapse. In Owens Valley, extensive groundwater pumping at city-owned wells has helped lower the water table and contribute to die-off of vegetation on portions of the valley floor. The shores of receding Mono Lake and the lakebed of Owens Lake—which dried up in the mid-1920s after Owens Valley water diversions began—are major sources of air pollution when alkali dust blows off their exposed surfaces.

In the late 1980s, Inyo County and the City of Los Angeles forged an out-of-court agreement that, if implemented, will ensure careful monitoring of groundwater use and substantially increase the surface flow of the lower Owens River. In 1989, a court order temporarily blocked further water diversions from Mono Basin streams, and the California State Legislature established a fund to help Los Angeles develop alternative water sources for the city.

Snow flurry over Mono Lake. WILLIAM NEILL

A Land of Year-Round Recreation

As farms and ranches vanished from Owens Valley during the 1920s and 1930s, community leaders looked to tourism to help revitalize the area's depressed economy. Led by *Inyo Register* publisher W. A. Chalfant and eastern California's traveling priest Father J. J. Crowley, Owens Valley promoters began to tout the Eastern Sierra as a year-round vacationland.

During the first decades of the century, Eastern Sierra tourism was impeded by the absence of all-weather highways into and through the region. When the road over Tioga Pass opened in 1915, it provided a key trans-Sierra link between Yosemite Valley and the Eastern Sierra; the route, however, wasn't paved until 1961. As early as 1910, the Inyo Good Roads Club, an Owens Valley association, urged state officials to build a highway along the east side of the Sierra. Their efforts proved successful, and in 1916 the first section of "El Camino Sierra," now part of U.S. 395, was completed on Sherwin Grade north of Bishop. Road construction proceeded in piecemeal fashion, and by 1931 a paved highway extended from Los Angeles to Bridgeport Valley.

Members of Hollywood's movie industry, some of whom had worked on films set in the Alabama Hills near Lone Pine, were among the first tourists to frequent the Eastern Sierra.

Climbers ascend Mt. Tom. ANDY SELTERS

Their enthusiasm for the area helped stimulate the growth of summer resort enclaves such as Big Pine Creek, Mammoth, and June Lake. With the advent of better roads, the region also attracted growing numbers of sportsmen, campers, and sightseers. Pack stations began operating near wilderness trailheads and helped open up the Sierra backcountry to visitors.

The introduction of ski tows along U.S. 395 in the mid-1930s began to draw winter tourists to the region. A modest ski operation began at Mammoth Mountain in 1941; this led to a dramatic increase in the numbers of winter visitors and opened the way for development of ski resorts at Mammoth Mountain and June Mountain during the 1950s and 1960s.

Since the 1970s, the phenomenal growth of sports such as backpacking, cross-country skiing, hang gliding, climbing, and bicycling has greatly contributed to the popularity of the Eastern Sierra as a vacation destination. The region now enjoys a national reputation as a beautiful and challenging setting for year-round outdoor recreation.

The Eastern Sierra encompasses some of California's most spectacular wildlands and offers an abundance of scenic, historic, and recreational resources. Once a source of heartbreak, the area's lack of development has become one of its greatest assets. Today, the Eastern Sierra is experiencing a period of prosperity based on tourism, a trend that has far exceeded the hopes of Chalfant, Crowley, and other early proponents of the region.

A pack train heads into the Mammoth backcountry. JIM STROUP

Paiute and Shoshone of the Eastern Sierra
by William H. Michael

The Paiutes had made their last stand at the border of the Bitter Lake; battle-driven they died in its waters, and the land filled with cattle-men and adventurers for gold . . .
—Mary Austin,
The Basket Maker

Paiute and Shoshone Indians had inhabited the Eastern Sierra for 1,000 to 1,500 years when the first whites arrived in the mid-19th century. At that time, as many as 2,000 Native Americans lived in the region extending from Little Lake (south of Owens Valley) to Bridgeport Valley. The Panamint Shoshone, part of the Western Shoshone whose traditional territory included much of Nevada and Utah, occupied desert lands to the south and east of Owens Lake. Owens Valley Paiute inhabited an area extending from Owens Lake to Round Valley (near Bishop). The Mono Lake Paiute lived to the north of Owens Valley, occupying the southern portion of the Northern Paiute territory, which extended into Oregon and Washington.

The Indians practiced an efficient and creative pattern of seasonal exploitation of the Eastern Sierra's rich resources. Owens Valley Paiute

Maggie Ross, Owens Valley Paiute. EASTERN CALIFORNIA MUSEUM / A.A. FORBES

harvested at least 40 different plant foods; the Northern Paiute utilized as many as 150. Other food resources included waterfowl, rabbits, deer, antelope, mountain sheep, fish, and insect pupae. These foods were procured from environments as diverse as the pinyon forests of the White and Inyo mountains and the brine-encrusted shores of Owens and Mono lakes.

In upper Owens Valley, Paiutes developed a system of agriculture by harnessing the abundance of Sierra streamwater to irrigate fields of edible

Owens Valley Pauite baskets on display in the Eastern California Museum. BILL EVARTS

plants. They developed a less transient lifestyle than other Great Basin Indians and established permanent communities. Separate dialects of the Paiute language evolved at the different Owens Valley villages.

The intrusion of whites into the Eastern Sierra in the 1860s had a devastating impact on the area's Indian population. Herds of cattle brought by ranchers grazed the meadows on the valley floors, destroying native grasses whose seeds provided a major food source for the Indians. Miners decimated high desert woodlands to fuel their smelters, eliminating vast tracts of pinyon pine and thereby depleting the pine nut crop which the Indians relied on for winter sustenance. Farmers burned grasslands and appropriated the Paiute's irrigation systems for their own crops. As indigenous food

Traditional Pauite dwelling, Owens Valley early 1900s. EASTERN CALIFORNIA MUSEUM / A.A. FORBES

sources were depleted and starvation set in, the Indians turned to the only food supply left—the ranchers' cattle.

It was inevitable that armed conflict would follow. In 1862 the soldiers of the Second Cavalry, California Volunteers, arrived to establish Camp Independence and restore order. One year later, the brutal forced removal of nearly 900 Paiute and Shoshone from their homeland to a reservation near Fort Tejon brought an end to the warfare.

In the years following their relocation, many Paiute and Shoshone left the Tejon area and returned to Owens Valley. They provided an important source of labor for the farms, ranches, and homes of the now dominant white community. By 1930 the City of Los Angeles had acquired 90% of the valley's farms and 85% of the property within the valley's communities for its aqueduct and water storage system. The local agricultural economy collapsed, and the exodus of the farmer destroyed the market for Indian labor. Once again, the area's Paiute and Shoshone were faced with uncertainty over their future.

During the early 1930s, the City of Los Angeles presented the U.S. Department of the Interior with a complex land swap proposal that would relocate and consolidate the Indian populations of Owens Valley. During congressional hearings on the subject, Johnny Symmes, an Owens Valley Paiute, presented this testimony to the Senate Committee on Indian Affairs:

> . . . once we Indians had our ways and had [our] own food and meat and we owned this Valley—Owens Valley. When the white people come they took everything from us and learned us how to work, and we worked for them. Now they took the work from us, and we are without work. We want work to be given us, we the Owens Valley Indians, right in Owens Valley.

The U.S. Congress approved reservations at Lone Pine, Big Pine, and Bishop in 1937. With no other options, many Indians abandoned their traditional homesites to resettle on the reservations. The Paiute community at Fort Independence did not agree to the proposed land exchanges, however, and still exists on lands set aside in 1915. Today, several Indian reservations are located between Lone Pine and Bridgeport. Each is governed by an elected tribal council and most have adopted constitutions.

In recent years, there has been a growing appreciation of Paiute and Shoshone cultural heritage in the Eastern Sierra. The Cultural Center on the Bishop Reservation houses excellent exhibits depicting traditional Paiute and Shoshone lifestyles; displays at the Eastern California Museum in Independence and the Mono County Museum in Bridgeport also feature the area's Native American culture. Although their traditional economy and communities were ravaged during the 19th century, the Indian people of the Eastern Sierra have managed to hold onto remnants of their ancestral lands and remain a strong presence in the region.

Lone Pine Region

How strange it seemed to be standing on the highest point in the United States, and looking off for a distance of seventy miles down into Death Valley, the lowest point!…Oh, what an inspiration it was to look from that magnificent peak on the grand panorama of mountains, reaching from beyond the Yosemite to San Bernardino! Range after range in every direction, peak on peak, comprising almost limitless forms, rise one above the other, each striving for the mastery. Stepping near the eastern edge, I looked down a sheer descent of three thousand feet on a small lakelet, partially covered with snow and ice. Still farther east lay Owens River Valley, with its sparkling lake, winding river, and golden fields of grain.

—Anna Mills,

Mt. Whitney Club Journal, 1902

Left: Golden trout, California's State Fish, is prized by backcountry anglers. PAT O'HARA
Opposite: The Alabama Hills and Lone Pine Peak. WILLARD CLAY

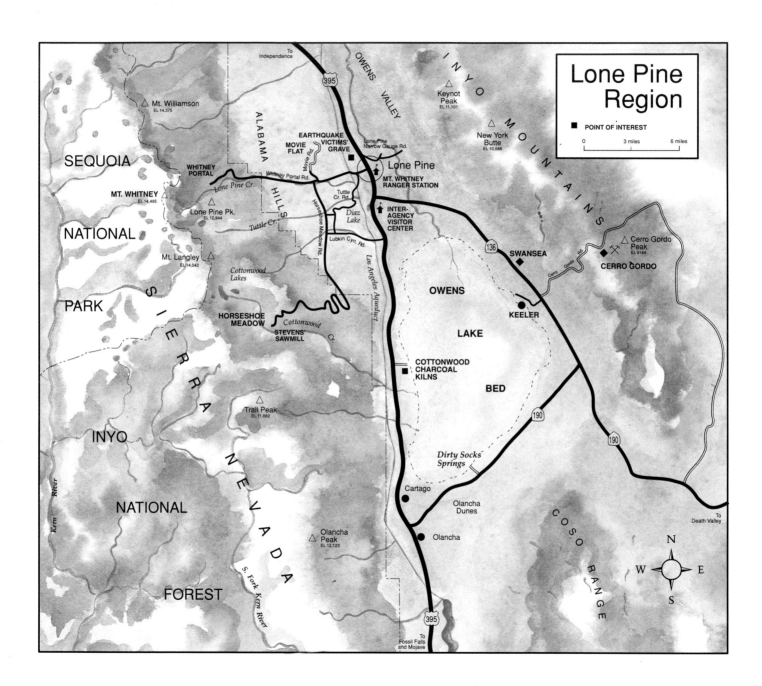

Lone Pine Region

■ POINT OF INTEREST

0   3 miles   6 miles

To
Independence

OWENS VALLEY

INYO MOUNTAINS

Mt. Williamson
EL 14,375

Keynot
Peak
EL 11,101

New York
Butte
EL 10,688

SEQUOIA

ALABAMA

EARTHQUAKE
MOVIE
FLAT

VICTIMS'
GRAVE

Lone Pine
Narrow Gauge Rd.

Lone Pine

WHITNEY
PORTAL

Movie Rd.

Whitney Portal Rd.

MT. WHITNEY
RANGER STATION

MT. WHITNEY
EL 14,495

Lone Pine Cr.

HILLS

Tuttle
Cr. Rd.

INTER-
AGENCY
VISITOR
CENTER

Lone Pine Pk.
EL 12,944

Horseshoe Meadow Rd.

Diaz
Lake

Cerro Gordo
Peak
EL 9184

NATIONAL

Tuttle Cr.

Lubkin Cyn. Rd.

136

SWANSEA

Cerro Gordo Rd.

CERRO GORDO

Mt. Langley
EL 14,042

Cottonwood
Lakes

Los Angeles Aqueduct

OWENS

KEELER

PARK

SIERRA

HORSESHOE
MEADOW

Cottonwood

STEVENS'
SAWMILL

LAKE

COTTONWOOD
CHARCOAL
KILNS

BED

INYO

Cottonwood
Cr.

Trail Peak
EL 11,662

190

Dirty Socks
Springs

NEVADA

190

NATIONAL

Kern River

Cartago

Olancha
Dunes

To
Death Valley

COSO RANGE

Olancha
Peak
EL 12,123

Olancha

N

FOREST

S. Fork Kern River

W   E

S

395

To
Fossil Falls
and Mojave

52   CALIFORNIA'S EASTERN SIERRA

Fossil Falls

Fossil Falls provides a vivid introduction to the Eastern Sierra's recent geologic and climatic history. Fossil Falls began forming about 20,000 years ago when volcanic eruptions in the Coso Range sent lava flows spilling into the southern Rose Valley and across the path of an ice-age river. Over time, the river carved a canyon through the lava bed, and as it cascaded south, the sediment-laden water scoured and polished the basalt. Following the ice age, the area's climate became more arid, and about 4,000 years ago, the ancient river ceased flowing through this channel, exposing a "fossilized waterfall."

Volcanic landforms abound near Fossil Falls. The trail to the "falls" winds through a field of craggy lava. Rising to the immediate north is Red Hill, a rusty-red cinder cone composed of porous rock called *scoria*. Cinder cones and lava flows are also visible in the Coso Range to the southeast. An impressive palisade of columnar basalt flanks the east side of U.S. 395 just a few miles south of Fossil Falls.

Although Fossil Falls lies within the province of the Mojave Desert, this region was not always arid. There are numerous reminders of human habitation from centuries past, when water and game were more abundant. Observant visitors may see obsidian chips, petroglyphs, grinding holes, or

Water-sculpted lava and the ancient river gorge at Fossil Falls. BILL EVARTS

wide circles of stones—the foundations of temporary shelters built by Shoshone Indians. All Native American artifacts are protected by law and should be left in place, undisturbed.

A short trail leads to an overlook at the edge of the Fossil Falls gorge. (Keep children back from the edge.) Visitors may enter the canyon for a closer look at this intricate maze of water-sculpted lava. The area is most colorful in spring, when delicate annual wildflowers bloom amidst the black, tumbled lava.

• **Fossil Falls**, *administered by the Bureau of Land Management, is located just east of U.S. 395 in southern Rose Valley. Exit the highway at Cinder Road (unpaved) 3 miles north of Little Lake or 5 miles south of the Coso Junction Rest Stop. Continue 1/2 mile east to a right curve and another 1/2 mile south to the parking area.*

The vast playa of Owens Lake, looking north at dusk. BILL EVARTS

Owens Lake

Until early in the 20th century, Owens Valley contained a large inland sea—Owens Lake. Tens of thousands of birds flocked to the lake during annual migrations, Paiute Indians harvested brine fly pupae along the shore in summer, and ore-carrying steamers plied its waters during the 1870s. Owens Lake is dry today, but the immense white and pastel playa that remains is an oddly beautiful landscape, appreciated more with each visit. Low dunes ring the lakebed's southern and eastern rim and provide quiet niches for contemplating the valley's vast skies and mountain ranges. Spring-fed ponds and marshes still attract many varieties of shorebirds and waterfowl.

The drying of Owens Lake can be attributed to both climatic changes and human intervention. Ancient Owens Lake was one of many Pleistocene lakes that filled low-lying basins of the western United States. It covered lower Owens Valley and at times extended north toward present-day Bishop. The climate became drier when the last ice age ended and Owens Lake, no longer replenished by runoff from massive snowfields and glaciers, began to recede. After the water level fell below the lake's outlet, fresh water no longer circulated and the lake became briny and alkaline.

When settlers first arrived in Owens Valley during the 1860s, the lake covered over 100 square miles and was 30 feet deep. It began shrinking at the turn of the century as a result of upstream water diversion by Owens Valley farmers; the lake was completely dry by the mid-1920s, a decade after the Los Angeles Aqueduct began diverting virtually all valley water away from the lake. Today, the lakebed accumulates enough moisture to support single-celled green algae; it also contains billions of bacterial organisms—halobacteria—that give it a pink-red tone. Strong winds often whip up a mile-high cloud of dust off the playa's dry salt flats, completely obscuring the view and polluting the air with alkali dust.

In contrast to the haunting quiet of today's playa, Owens Lake was the hub of a transportation network during the mining heyday at Cerro Gordo in the nearby Inyo Mountains. A steady stream of wagons rounded the north shore of the lake, hauling silver down from the mines and returning with provisions and equipment. Civil War veteran Colonel Sherman Stevens built a silver- and lead-smelting furnace at Swansea on the lake's northeast shore in 1869. In 1873, Stevens' smelter manager, James Brady, launched an 85-foot steamboat, the *Bessie Brady*, and began transporting silver ingots from Swansea to Cartago on the lake's southwest shore. Stevens' own steamer, the *Molly Stevens*, began navigating the lake's waters in 1877.

By 1878, the silver economy at Cerro Gordo had collapsed and the Owens Lake steamboat era came to an end. Expecting a revival of the Inyo Mountain mines, the Owens Lake Mining and Milling Company unveiled ambitious plans for a new lakefront town in 1880. The community, named

Keeler, became the southern terminus for the narrow-gauge Carson & Colorado Railroad in 1883. After the turn of the century, Keeler experienced a period of modest but short-lived prosperity when Cerro Gordo's mines were reworked for zinc and lead production.

Cottonwood Charcoal Kilns:
In 1873, Colonel Stevens began providing wood for Cerro Gordo's smelters from his sawmill on Cottonwood Creek high in the Sierra Nevada. Cordwood and lumber were sent down Cottonwood Canyon through a nine-mile flume that ended near the lake—some 6,000 feet below the sawmill. To process wood into charcoal, Stevens built two adobe-brick kilns near the lakeshore in 1876-77. The lumber and charcoal were ferried across Owens Lake on the *Bessie Brady* and the *Molly Stevens* and then hauled by mule-drawn wagon another nine miles and 5,000 feet up to Cerro Gordo. The large, beehive-shaped kilns, much eroded over time, are still standing.

Swansea: On the west side of Highway 136, a California Historic Landmark and stone ruins mark the site of the Owens Lake Silver-Lead Company and the wharf for the *Bessie Brady*. The site of James Brady's residence (private property) is on the east side of the road.

Sierra cordwood was sent by flume to these adobe kilns, made into charcoal, and shipped by steamer across Owens Lake to Cerro Gordo's silver smelters. BILL EVARTS

American avocets above Dirty Socks Springs, Owens Lake. BILL EVARTS

Keeler: Keeler is home to a handful of residents and contains an abandoned talc-processing plant. The picturesque Carson & Colorado railroad station (now a private residence) is found near the center of this desert hamlet. Cerro Gordo Road intersects Highway 136 just east of town.

Dirty Socks Springs: The warm, artesian springs that bubble to the surface here have attracted travelers for many years. A cement swimming pool built in 1927 is all that remains of various efforts to develop the site for recreational use. Dirty Socks is a good bird-watching locale (look for American avocet) and offers fine vistas of the Owens Lake playa and southeastern Sierra peaks.

• *Marked by a California Historic Landmark sign on U.S. 395, the turnoff to the **Cottonwood Charcoal Kilns** is on the east side of the highway, 11.5 miles south of Lone Pine or 10 miles north of Olancha. A good dirt road continues 1 mile east to the kilns.* **Swansea** *is on Highway 136, 10 miles east of the U.S. 395/Highway 136 junction (just south of Lone Pine), or 22.5 miles from Olancha via Highways 190 and 136.* **Keeler** *is on Highway 136, 13 miles southeast of the 395/136 junction, or 19.5 miles from Olancha via Highways 190 and 136. The turnoff to **Dirty Socks Springs** is on Highway 190, 28 miles from Lone Pine via Highways 136 and 190, or 5 miles east of Olancha on Highway 190. Turn north where overhead power lines cross the highway; the springs are a short distance from the highway.*

Cerro Gordo

If the rugged landscape of the southern Inyo Mountains seems remote and inhospitable today, one can only imagine how isolated it was when Mexican prospector Pablo Flores found silver here in 1865. The site of Flores' discovery, named *Cerro Gordo* (Spanish for "Fat Hill") became the most productive silver-mining district in California history. By some estimates Cerro Gordo's mines yielded more than $13 million in silver, lead, and zinc—an amount rivaled only by Nevada's famous Comstock Lode. Although Cerro Gordo was virtually abandoned by 1880, a number of its original buildings are still standing and, with the exception of Bodie, it is the best-preserved ghost town in eastern California.

Cerro Gordo's silver-mining era is a major chapter in Owens Valley history, and beginning in the late 1860s the wealth of its mines helped transform Los Angeles from a small coastal town into a prosperous commercial center. Virtually all of Cerro Gordo's silver-lead ingots were transported in mule-drawn wagons across the Mojave Desert and over the coastal mountains to Los Angeles' seaport of San Pedro, where they were shipped to a San Francisco refinery. The Cerro Gordo Freighting Company was spending over $1,000 a day in Los Angeles on provisions to carry back to Cerro Gordo—at that time a very sizable sum. The *Los Angeles News* proclaimed: "What Los Angeles is, is mainly due to it [Cerro Gordo]. It is the silver cord that binds our present existence."

In 1868, San Francisco mining expert Mortimer Belshaw and two partners established the Union Mining Company, an operation that was to dominate Cerro Gordo during its peak years. The shrewd and capable Belshaw built an eight-mile toll road, the Yellow Grade Road, up the steep 5,000-foot ascent from Owens Valley.

Cerro Gordo's American Hotel, built during the 1860s silver-mining boom. BILL EVARTS

that year when teamster Remi Nadeau contracted with mine owners to ship their silver from the dock at Cartago to Los Angeles. Nadeau's operation, which employed 50 mule trains, delivered silver to Los Angeles around the clock.

Despite the gigantic silver boom of the early 1870s, declining production and increasing costs eventually forced the Cerro Gordo mine owners to cease operations. Belshaw shut down his once-prolific smelter in 1876, and by 1878 "Fat Hill" was fast becoming a ghost town. Cerro Gordo experienced a number of modest revivals— including a successful zinc operation from 1911 to 1915—but it never

He also devised an efficient blast furnace that vastly increased smelter output, ensuring rapid production of silver ingots from the mountain's rich ore.

Cerro Gordo was continually plagued with transportation and logistics problems. Fuel for the smelter furnaces was scarce. The local hillsides were virtually stripped of pinyon and juniper by 1874, and firewood and charcoal were carried in from many miles away. Until 1870, the town's water supply was hauled in by wagons and burro pack trains. Travel around Owens Lake and along Cerro Gordo's steep toll road was slow and laborious,

and teamsters took three weeks to complete the 440-mile round-trip journey to Los Angeles.

James Brady, then manager of the Swansea silver-lead smelter at Owens Lake, built an 85-foot steamboat, the *Bessie Brady,* in 1873. His steamer ferried bullion across the lake to Cartago, eliminating the arduous wagon trip around the lake's north shore and shaving several days off the trip to Los Angeles. Still, available transport could not keep pace with smelter production, and thousands of silver ingots piled up on lakeside docks. Cerro Gordo's freighting problems were finally alleviated later

Cemetery outside Keeler. BILL EVARTS

surpassed its 1870s heyday when thousands of miners, merchants, and laborers were lured to its rich silver mines. Today, Cerro Gordo is undergoing a revival of a different sort as its historic mine buildings, hotels, homes, and stores are being restored by private owners.

• *A steep, narrow, 8-mile dirt road ascends to **Cerro Gordo**, just southeast of Keeler on Highway 136. The scenic drive climbs past Joshua trees and juniper before reaching the ghost town, perched at 8,500 feet. This trip is not recommended for vehicles with automatic transmissions. Also, carry extra water for your car radiator. Cerro Gordo is privately owned and visitors should make an advance appointment for a tour of the site. For current information, check with the Eastern Sierra InterAgency Visitor Center in Lone Pine.*

Horseshoe Meadow

Located at one of the highest roadends in the Sierra Nevada, Horseshoe Meadow is a beautiful destination for a picnic, day hike, or fishing expedition. The trip to Horseshoe Meadow is worth making for the drive alone. The paved road climbs almost 6,000 feet from the desert floor at Lone Pine to a subalpine setting near 10,000 feet, and it offers breathtaking vistas of Owens Valley, the Inyo Mountains, and

Cottonwood Creek meanders through beautiful Horseshoe Meadow. BILL EVARTS

distant ranges of the Mojave Desert. Flora and fauna endemic to the southern Sierra flourish near Horseshoe Meadow, including foxtail pine and golden trout.

The meadow's superb wildflower display is best in late spring or early summer, when carpets of shooting star come into bloom. Bird watchers are likely to spot a variety of species, including Clark's nutcracker, mountain bluebird, and possibly a golden eagle. Trails lead to the adjacent Golden Trout Wilderness, the John Muir Wilderness, and Sequoia National Park. Cottonwood Lakes Basin, a gentle, alpine landscape

dotted with lakes and meadows, is a 12-mile round-trip hike from the parking area.

Golden trout, California's state fish, can be easily seen in Cottonwood Creek, which meanders through Horseshoe Meadow. Native to the upper Kern River of the southern Sierra, golden trout were first introduced to the eastern side of the range by Colonel Sherman Stevens in 1876. He carried 13 goldens in a tea pot from Mulkey Creek (a tributary of the Kern River) and released them at Horseshoe Meadow. Today golden trout are protected by special fishing regulations.

Foxtail pine, *Pinus balfouriana*, is found throughout the Horseshoe Meadow area. This conifer occurs only in the southern Sierra Nevada and in a few locales in northwestern California. A picturesque, hardy tree, foxtail pine usually grows in scattered groves on exposed, rocky slopes near timberline. It can be recognized by its tapered shape and dark, reddish-brown bark. The tree's dense, parallel-running needles give each branch tip the bushy appearance of a fox's tail.

Horseshoe Meadow Road passes the ruins of a sawmill that operated at the head of Cottonwood Canyon from 1873 to 1878. Built by Colonel Stevens, the mill supplied cordwood and lumber to the mining operations at Cerro Gordo, across Owens Valley to the east. Stevens had a ready-made market for his product because the southern Inyo Mountains had been all but stripped of timber to fuel Cerro Gordo's wood-burning smelters. From the sawmill, wood was sent bobbing down a nine-mile flume to the base of the Sierra. It was then hauled by wagon to Stevens' wharf at Cottonwood Landing, transported by steamer across Owens Lake, and reloaded onto wagons for the steep climb to Cerro Gordo.

• The route to **Horseshoe Meadow** is *open May through October, depending on snowfall. From Lone Pine, drive 3.5 miles west on Whitney Portal Road, turn south*

Top: Site of Stevens' sawmill. BILL EVARTS
Bottom: Hang gliders preparing to launch from Walt's Point. BILL EVARTS

on Horseshoe Meadow Road, and continue 21 miles to the roadend. The road forks near its end; the meadow is a short walk from the picnic area located on the south (left) fork. The ruins of **Stevens' Sawmill** *are located about 100 yards southeast of Horseshoe Meadow Road, 22.5 miles southwest of Lone Pine,*

or 2 miles from Horseshoe Meadow. Walt's Point, located on Horseshoe Meadow Road about 21 miles from Lone Pine (4 miles from the roadend), is a launching site for world class long-distance hang glider flights.

Eastern Sierra InterAgency Visitor Center

The Eastern Sierra InterAgency Visitor Center provides information, exhibits, maps, brochures, and what is probably the most comprehensive selection of books on the Eastern Sierra. The center offers for sale more than 300 titles covering the natural and cultural history of the Sierra Nevada, Great Basin, and Mojave Desert regions. Displays include information on desert safety and the wilderness ethic, a small rock and mineral collection, and, outside, a small native plant garden. From its shaded picnic tables, visitors can enjoy views south and east to the Coso and Inyo ranges and west to Mount Whitney and the Sierra. Demonstrating a degree of participation unique among interagency visitor centers, some nine agencies from all levels of government—city, county, state, and federal—cooperate in its operation.

• *The* **Eastern Sierra InterAgency Visitor Center** *is located at the junction of U.S. 395 and Highway 136, about 1 mile south of Lone Pine.*

Golden Trout

Golden trout, California's state fish, are found in about 300 lakes and 700 miles of streams in the high country of the Sierra Nevada. Unlike other trout, goldens are stocked almost exclusively in wilderness areas, and anglers must head into the backcountry to find them. The only location in the eastern Sierra Nevada accessible by automobile where you can observe or fish for golden trout is Cottonwood Creek in Horseshoe Meadow, a 25-mile drive southwest of Lone Pine.

Native to the upper Kern River drainage of the southern Sierra, golden trout are probably descendants of a population of rainbow trout that, many centuries ago, became physically isolated from other trout and evolved separately. The brightly colored goldens are considered the most beautiful of all trout. They have a dark olive back, olive to golden-yellow sides, an orange-red belly and side stripe, and white-tipped fins. There are two forms of golden trout: Little Kern and Volcano Creek (also known as the South Fork Kern). The Volcano Creek golden trout, distinguished by fewer spots and more vivid color, is widespread; the Little Kern golden trout is largely restricted to the drainage of the Little Kern River.

In the mid-1800s, golden trout existed in only a handful of streams in

Little Kern golden trout. B. "MOOSE" PETERSON

the upper Kern River drainage. In 1876 Colonel Sherman Stevens completed the first successful transplant of golden trout when he captured 13 goldens in Mulkey Creek in the Kern drainage, transported them over the Sierra crest, and released them in Cottonwood Creek. The trout thrived in their new environment, and descendants of Sherman's original 13 goldens were planted in the Cottonwood Lakes in 1891. Located in the John Muir Wilderness, the Cottonwood Lakes are California's only source of pure-strain golden trout eggs for hatchery rearing.

It is difficult to breed goldens in captivity. Rather than relying on broodstock, California Department of Fish and Game fish culturalists gather golden trout eggs from the

Cottonwood Lakes each spring and transport them to incubators at Hot Creek State Fish Hatchery near Mammoth Lakes. After hatching, golden trout fry (baby fish) are reared in hatchery troughs. By late summer they have developed into fingerlings and are air-dropped into backcountry lakes. When this fisheries program began operation in 1917, all backcountry planting was done by pack mule. Aerial planting began after WW II and dramatically expanded the range of the golden trout in the high Sierra.

Although efforts to extend its range have been successful, the state fish faces challenges to survival in its native waters. Interbreeding with introduced rainbow trout threatens the Little Kern golden trout, and it was added to the U.S. Fish and Wildlife Service Endangered Species List in 1977. To assist the Little Kern goldens, an interagency group is systematically replacing hybrids and non-native species with pure golden strains in many streams of the Little Kern River drainage. The California Department of Fish and Game and the Forest Service are also endeavoring to remove the exotic brown trout and to restore damaged riparian habitat in the drainages of the South Fork of the Kern and Little Kern.

Mt. Williamson and an amphitheater of boulders in the Alabama Hills. BILL EVARTS

Natural arch, Alabama Hills. BILL EVARTS

Alabama Hills

The Alabama Hills have enchanted Eastern Sierra visitors for over a century, attracting 19th-century prospectors, Hollywood filmmakers, and countless artists and photographers. Today, they offer a captivating setting for recreation: dozens of dirt roads and trails wind among the boulders, paths hug the banks of Tuttle and Lone Pine creeks, and rock outcrops frame stunning vistas of Mount Whitney, the Sierra's eastern escarpment, and the western face of the Inyo Mountains. During spring, the area is splashed with color by desert wildflowers such as Mojave aster, apricot mallow, and desert paintbrush.

This rugged wonderland of boulders rises abruptly from Owens Valley just west of Lone Pine. Although the Alabama Hills' golden-brown rocks present a vivid contrast to the jagged gray spires of nearby Sierra peaks, they are nearly identical to the Sierra Nevada in geologic age and composition. The difference in their appearance can be attributed to differing weathering processes.

Geologists theorize that the granite of the Alabama Hills was shaped by chemical weathering during a period when the climate was more moist and the rock was covered with soil. Chemical weathering, promoted by the downward percolation of water, exploited the granite's system of vertical and horizontal joints (zones of

Cottonwoods and willows mark the path of Tuttle Creek in the Alabama Hills. BILL EVARTS

In contrast, the peaks of the high Sierra have been shaped predominantly by mechanical weathering. Their granite is repeatedly subjected to freezing and thawing temperatures; as rainwater or snowmelt freezes and expands in the granite's joints, it weakens and eventually fractures the rock. This process steadily exposes fresh surfaces and contributes to the Sierra's sharp, chiseled features.

The Alabama Hills haven't always been the recreational haven one finds today. In March 1862, settlers attacked a Paiute camp here, killing 11 people before the Indians could take cover among the rocks. The hills derive their name from a local mining claim, which was dubbed "The Alabama"—in honor of the famous Confederate battleship—by prospectors sympathetic to the Confederacy. Several Owens Valley locations were later named "Kearsarge" for the Union ship that sank the *Alabama*.

Cinematographers discovered the Alabama Hills in the 1920s. For several decades Hollywood studios took advantage of this powerful setting to film scores of movie classics, including *Wagon Train*, *Gunga Din*, and *Lives of a Bengal Lancer*.

The Bureau of Land Management has designated 30,000 acres here as the "Alabama Hills Recreation Lands." There are two primary routes into the area: these are Movie Road and Tuttle Creek Road.

weakness that develop as granitic magma cools), separating the bedrock into blocks, then rounding off their edges and corners. As the climate became drier, soil formation slowed and erosion eventually stripped away the soil mantle, exposing the boulder piles we see today. Chemical weathering continues to shape the Alabama Hills, although in the present arid climate it proceeds at a slower rate.

Movie Flat: A graded dirt road leads across Movie Flat, where many well-known Westerns have been filmed. Roads and trails fan out among the marvelous boulder piles that surround the flat. The low hills to the northeast of Movie Flat offer splendid views of Sierra peaks, including Mount Whitney and Lone Pine Peak.

Tuttle Creek: This pleasant (but steep and narrow) motoring route winds through the Alabama Hills along the banks of Tuttle Creek. It is not recommended for large RVs or vehicles pulling trailers.

• *The **Alabama Hills** lie just west of Lone Pine. To reach **Movie Flat**, turn west on Whitney Portal Road in central Lone Pine and drive 2.8 miles to Movie Road. Turn north (right) and continue about 1 mile. Begin the **Tuttle Creek** tour in central Lone Pine. Travel 1/2 mile west on Whitney Portal Road, turn south (left) on Tuttle Creek Road, and continue 4.1 miles up Tuttle Creek Road to Sunset. Turn west (right) on Sunset and intersect Horseshoe Meadow Road after 1/1 mile. Turn right on Horseshoe Meadow Road, which then reconnects with Whitney Portal Road, returning you past Movie Road to Lone Pine.*

Above: Cacti and desert flowers in the Alabama Hills. GALEN ROWELL / MOUNTAIN LIGHT
Left: The Alabama Hills' blocks of granite were separated and rounded by the work of chemical weathering during a time when they were covered with soil. BILL EVARTS

Mount Whitney

The towering Sierra crest west of Lone Pine is one of the most majestic sights in California. Mount Whitney crowns the Sierra Nevada, and its 14,495-foot summit is the highest point in the contiguous United States. Just 80 aerial miles east lies the lowest point in North America—Badwater, in Death Valley National Monument, 283 feet *below* sea level. In the course of a few hours, one can drive from Death Valley's desert sink to the base of Mount Whitney's granite ramparts— a unique journey that provides travelers an opportunity to view the lowest and highest topography in the lower 48 states.

Although Mount Whitney rises 10,000 feet above Owens Valley, it is flanked by other tall mountains and is difficult to pick out. Lone Pine Peak, set east of the main escarpment, appears larger and more imposing from the valley floor and is often mistaken for Mount Whitney. The grounds of the Eastern Sierra Inter-Agency Visitor Center, located just south of Lone Pine, offer a good view of Mount Whitney. The classic, head-on view of the peak is seen from the town of Lone Pine; for an unob-structed view, drive a few miles west on Whitney Portal Road through the Alabama Hills.

Members of the California State Geological Survey identified Mount Whitney as the nation's highest peak

in the summer of 1864. Led by William Brewer, the expedition conducted the first complete study of the state's topography and natural resources. As the party of surveyors began exploring the more remote sections of the Sierra Nevada—moving east through what is now Sequoia National Park—they were surprised and awestruck by the gallery of giant peaks they encountered. Brewer wrote: "Such a landscape! A hundred peaks in sight over thirteen thousand feet—many very sharp—deep canyons, cliffs in every direction . . ." Survey members Clarence King and Richard Cotter were the first to sight a huge, flat-topped peak that they thought—and later confirmed—to be the highest point in the nation. The group enthusiastically named this peak after the director of their survey, Josiah Dwight Whitney, the first California State Geologist.

From the moment Clarence King set eyes on Mount Whitney, he vowed to climb it. His first attempt failed, and it was seven years before King again made his way to the southern Sierra. Then, in the summer of 1871, he successfully ascended what he thought to be Mount Whitney. Much to his embarrassment, King learned two years later that he had climbed a 14,000-foot peak several miles south of his goal. He lost no time returning to California to ascend the actual Mount Whitney, only to find that a

Above. Mt. Whitney from Lower Boy Scout Lake, N. Fork of Lone Pine Creek. JEFF GNASS
Opposite: Viewing Mt. Whitney from the Alabama Hills. DAVID MUENCH

month earlier, on August 18, 1873, three fishermen on an outing from Lone Pine to the upper Kern River had already reached the summit. Inyo County residents lobbied to have the mountain renamed "Fishermen's Peak," but the proposal was defeated by the State Congress. That same year, John Muir climbed Mount Whitney and became the first person to reach the summit by climbing the peak's

Moonrise at the 14,495-foot summit of Mt. Whitney. GALEN ROWELL / MOUNTAIN LIGHT

stark eastern face. Muir's route, known today as the "Mountaineer's Route," is a challenging approach and is not part of the Mount Whitney Trail.

The Sierra high country remained remote and largely unexplored through the late 1800s; the sport of mountaineering was still in its infancy and interest in climbing Mount Whitney grew slowly. But by 1880, several more parties—some including women—had made ascents of Mount Whitney. Professor Samuel Langley led the first scientific expedition up the mountain in 1881. Lone Pine citizens financed and built the Mount Whitney Trail in 1904 to help accommodate the growing number of scientists who were interested in conducting astronomical and climatological research atop Mount Whitney. To provide shelter for the researchers and protect their scientific instruments, a stone hut was constructed in 1909; it stands at the summit to this day. To further accommodate visitors and scientists, the Whitney Portal Road was built by the Civilian Conservation Corps; it was completed in 1936.

Each year over 10,000 people of all ages and nationalities are issued permits to climb Mount Whitney. The 22-mile round-trip hike to the summit is rigorous, and less than half of those who attempt to climb Mount Whitney actually sign in at the top. Climbers and campers should contact the Mount Whitney Ranger Station before March 1st for summer reservations, since permits are required and the number of daily climbers is limited.

The trailhead for Mount Whitney is located at Whitney Portal. Although intervening cliffs and forest block the view of the peak at the roadend, Whitney Portal is a delightful spot to sample the splendor of the Eastern Sierra. Whitney Portal's picnic area and trout pond are adjacent to Lone Pine Creek, which cascades past sheer walls of granite and magnificent specimens of red fir and Jeffrey pine.

• **Mount Whitney** *is due west of Lone Pine. To reach* **Whitney Portal,** *take Whitney Portal Road west from central Lone Pine and continue 13 miles to the roadend. Whitney Portal Road is normally open May to October, but access depends upon snow conditions.*

Earthquake Victims' Grave

At 2:30 in the morning, March 26, 1872, the jolt and sway of a powerful earthquake shook Owens Valley, destroying buildings and knocking fleeing residents off their feet. The massive tremor was felt from Mexico to Canada and as far east as Salt Lake City, Utah. John Muir, who experienced the earthquake in Yosemite Valley, over 100 miles away, wrote: "I was awakened by a tremendous earthquake, and though I had never before enjoyed a storm of this sort, the strange thrilling motion could not be mistaken, and I ran out of my cabin, both glad and frightened, shouting, 'A noble earthquake! A noble earthquake!' feeling sure I was going to learn something."

Seismographs had not yet been invented, but geologists estimate the earthquake's magnitude was between 8.0 and 8.3 on the Richter scale—of intensity equal to or greater than the San Francisco earthquake of 1906. In Lone Pine, at least 27 people were killed –buried beneath the rubble of unreinforced adobe structures—in what was then the most devastating earthquake in California history. Sixteen of these victims share a common grave near Lone Pine, now designated a California Historic Landmark.

Extensive damage was reported throughout Owens Valley, including the collapse of the Inyo County Courthouse in Independence. Lone Pine was nearly leveled; only 7 of its 59 buildings were left standing. The earthquake produced numerous scarps (short cliffs formed by vertical faulting) between Olancha and Big Pine, set off a *tsunami* ("tidal wave") on Owens Lake, and triggered massive avalanches in the Sierra. South of Lone Pine, sunken terrain between two quake fractures filled with water to become Diaz Lake. Springs dried up in Big Pine and new ones bubbled to the surface elsewhere. The earth beneath Owens Lake tilted slightly to the south, leaving a newly built pier on the north shore at Swansea high and dry.

• *The* **Earthquake Victims' Grave** *is located on the west side of U.S. 395 at the north end of Lone Pine. The grave rests on a fault scarp that predates the 1872 earthquake. From the site, look southwest toward the base of the Alabama Hills to spot a rock-strewn scarp that was formed by several earthquakes, including the 1872 tremor. The less-weathered rock along the scarp is lighter than its surroundings. Diaz Lake, now a recreation area, is about 2 miles south of Lone Pine on the west side of U.S. 395.*

The earth shifted 17 vertical feet along this fault scarp west of Lone Pine during the powerful earthquake of 1872. BILL EVARTS

Independence Region

The country where you may have sight and touch of that which is written lies between the high Sierras south from Yosemite—east and south over a very great assemblage of broken ranges.... the real heart and core of the country are not to be come at in a month's vacation. One must summer and winter with the land and wait its occasions. Pine woods that take two and three seasons to the ripening of cones, roots that lie by in the sand seven years awaiting a growing rain, firs that grow fifty years before flowering—these do not scrape acquaintance. But if ever you come beyond the borders as far as the town that lies in a hill dimple at the foot of Kearsarge, never leave it until you have knocked at the door of the brown house under the willow-tree at the end of the village street, and there you shall have such news of the land, of its trails and what is astir in them, as one lover of it can give to another.

—Mary Austin,
The Land of Little Rain, *1903*

Left: Streamside wildflowers in the Sierra backcountry. CHUCK PLACE
Opposite: Boulder-strewn alluvial fans south of Independence, near the base of 14,375-foot Mt. Williamson. BILL EVARTS

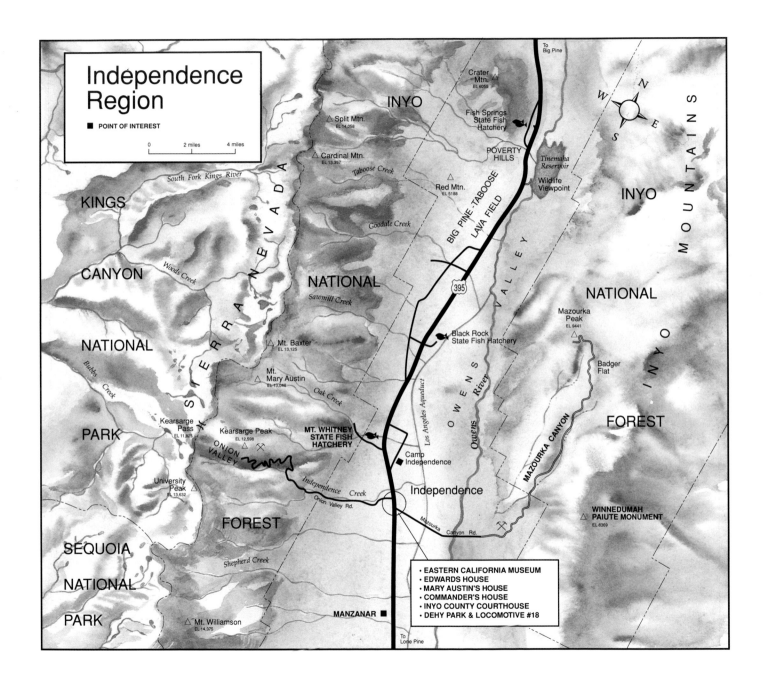

Independence Region

■ POINT OF INTEREST

0   2 miles   4 miles

KINGS

CANYON

NATIONAL

PARK

SEQUOIA

NATIONAL

PARK

S I E R R A   N E V A D A

South Fork Kings River

Woods Creek

Bubbs Creek

△ Split Mtn.
EL 14,058

△ Cardinal Mtn.
EL 13,397

Taboose Creek

Goodale Creek

NATIONAL

Sawmill Creek

△ Mt. Baxter
EL 13,125

Mt.
△ Mary Austin
EL 13,048

Oak Creek

Kearsarge
Pass
EL 11,825

Kearsarge Peak
EL 12,598
△ ✕

ONION
VALLEY

University
Peak △
EL 13,632

FOREST

Independence Creek

Onion Valley Rd.

Shepherd Creek

△ Mt. Williamson
EL 14,375

INYO

Crater
Mtn. △
EL 6058

Fish Springs
State Fish
Hatchery 🐟

POVERTY
HILLS

Red Mtn.
△ EL 5188

BIG PINE - TABOOSE LAVA FIELD

To Big Pine

Tinemaha
Reservoir

Wildlife
Viewpoint

395

🐟 Black Rock
State Fish Hatchery

Los Angeles Aqueduct

MT. WHITNEY
STATE FISH
HATCHERY 🐟

Camp
■ Independence

Independence

O W E N S   V A L L E Y

Owens River

Mazourka Canyon Rd.

Mazourka
Peak
△ EL 9441

Badger
Flat

MAZOURKA CANYON

INYO

INYO

NATIONAL

FOREST

I N Y O   M O U N T A I N S

WINNEDUMAH
△ PAIUTE MONUMENT
EL 8369

✕

MANZANAR ■

To
Lone Pine

- EASTERN CALIFORNIA MUSEUM
- EDWARDS HOUSE
- MARY AUSTIN'S HOUSE
- COMMANDER'S HOUSE
- INYO COUNTY COURTHOUSE
- DEHY PARK & LOCOMOTIVE #18

Manzanar

Shortly after the Japanese attack on Pearl Harbor, a site in Owens Valley was selected for the nation's first wartime internment camp. Rows of barracks were hastily erected on a barren tract of land between Lone Pine and Independence and, in March 1942, Manzanar Relocation Camp opened—the first of 10 internment centers that would imprison thousands of people of Japanese ancestry during World War II.

The most populous settlement in the history of Owens Valley, Manzanar had its own hospital, auditorium, schools, and workshops. The camp was surrounded by tall barbed-wire fences, and its residents were kept under constant surveillance by armed guards stationed in eight 50-foot towers. At its peak, the population of Manzanar Relocation Camp was over 10,000. By the time it officially closed in November 1945, over 11,000 people had resided there.

The camp derived its name from the small farming colony of Manzanar—Spanish for "apple orchard"—which was founded here in 1905 and thrived until the Los Angeles Aqueduct claimed local waters in the early 1920s. Once famous for their apple and pear orchards, Manzanar's fields flourished again when the internees cultivated decorative gardens, acres of vegetables, and the greens of a nine-hole golf course. Although few traces of the camp are visible, visitors who wish to explore the site can still find walls, foundations, and the remains of some of the internees' rock gardens. Manzanar serves as a somber reminder of the tragic and controversial decision by the U.S. government to intern thousands of Japanese Americans during World War II, and it is registered as both a State and National Historic Landmark; the National Park Service is studying plans to develop it as a national historic site. Rare photographs depicting life at Manzanar are part of a poignant exhibit at the Eastern California Museum in Independence.

• The main entrance to **Manzanar** is on the west side of U.S. 395, 6.3 miles south of Independence or 9 miles north of Lone Pine; it is marked by two stone guardhouses with pagoda-style roofs. Several

Above: Manzanar Cemetery. CARR CLIFTON
Opposite: A stone guardhouse on U.S. 395 marks the entrance to Manzanar. BILL EVARTS

hundred yards north of the entrance is Manzanar's auditorium, now an Inyo County maintenance garage. To reach Manzanar's cemetery, turn west onto an unmarked dirt road 0.8 miles north of the main entrance; after nearly a mile, this road curves south and the cemetery's white obelisk monument comes into view. The cemetery is the focal point of a memorial pilgrimage each April

Independence / Eastern California Museum

An ideal place to become acquainted with Eastern Sierra history is Independence, a small, picturesque community in the heart of Owens Valley. For 125 years Independence has been the seat of government for sprawling Inyo County, a rugged, sparsely populated region whose incredible topography includes both Mount Whitney and Death Valley—highest and lowest points in the contiguous United States. Independence is the home of Inyo County's Eastern California Museum and also contains a number of historic buildings, including the Edwards House (oldest structure in Owens Valley), the Inyo County Courthouse, and the home of Mary Austin, an early 20th-century author, naturalist, and feminist.

Eastern California Museum: This museum was established in 1928 to preserve, promote, and research the region's history; in 1969, it came under the management of Inyo County. The compact facility features both natural and cultural history, with exhibits on subjects such as Owens Valley pioneer days, the Carson & Colorado Railroad, Inyo County's 19th-century mining operations, and the construction of the Los Angeles Aqueduct.

The museum's collection of Paiute and Shoshone artifacts, including baskets, beadwork, and garments, is one of the finest in the West. Rare photographs, diagrams, and mementos are part of an evocative exhibit that chronicles the story of Manzanar Relocation Camp. Displays also honor two notable Eastern Sierra residents: mountaineer Norman Clyde and author Mary Austin. Outside, the museum displays antique wagons, tractors, and mining implements. A Paiute dwelling (*toni*) and Little Pine Village, a reconstructed pioneer town, are also found on museum grounds.

Edwards House: In 1863, Thomas Edwards purchased Putnam's Trading Post, the first permanent habitation in Inyo County (ca.1861). Three years later, Edwards laid out and patented the townsite of Independence. Although the Putnam cabin no longer exists, Edwards' residence (ca. 1863) is still standing and is the oldest building in Owens Valley.

Commander's House: The Commander's House was built in 1872 at Camp Independence, a military outpost located two miles north of the town of Independence. The Homestead-style structure was moved to its present site when Camp Independence closed in 1887. The interior has been decorated with 19th-century furnishings and is open to the

Top: "Little Pine Village" is a popular attraction at the Eastern California Museum. BILL EVARTS
Bottom: Built in 1872, the Commander's House is located in Independence. BILL EVARTS

Mary Austin's house in Independence, where she wrote The Land of Little Rain *in 1903.* BILL EVARTS

short stories, and numerous poems, plays, and articles. Her first book, *Land of Little Rain*, is considered a classic of desert literature; she wrote it in 1903 while living at this house in Independence.

Dehy Park / Locomotive #18: The retired #18 steam locomotive resides in the pleasant setting of Dehy Park on the banks of Independence Creek. The locomotive served the Carson & Colorado Railroad, a narrow-gauge freight and passenger line that operated in Owens Valley until 1960.

*• The **Eastern California Museum** is three blocks west of U.S. 395, at the intersection of Center and Grant streets. The museum is open Wednesday through Monday from 10 a.m. to 4 p.m. It is closed on Tuesday. Admission is free. The **Edwards House** (not open to the public) is located at 124 Market St., behind the Post Office. **Mary Austin's** House is at 253 Market St. The **Commander's House** is on the corner of Main and U.S. 395. The **Inyo County Courthouse** is on the east side of U.S. 395 near the center of town. **Dehy Park and Locomotive #18** are at the north end of Independence on the west side of U.S. 395. A pleasant walking tour can include all of the above destinations, which are located within a few blocks of one another.*

public on weekends from Memorial Day through Labor Day.

Inyo County Courthouse: Following heated debate among the area's citizens, Independence was chosen as the seat of government for Inyo County in 1866. It won out over Kearsarge and Bend City, then-populous mining towns that were virtually abandoned a decade later.

The first Inyo County Courthouse was destroyed in 1872 by the Lone Pine earthquake; the second burned in 1886. A third was considered too small, and it was replaced in 1923 by today's venerable structure.

Mary Austin's House: Writer, schoolteacher, and self-taught naturalist, Mary Austin (1868-1934) wrote 9 novels, 12 works of nonfiction, 50

Independence Creek cascades through Onion Valley, 5,000 feet above the Owens Valley floor. BILL EVARTS

Onion Valley

Onion Valley is nestled in a glacial canyon near the headwaters of Independence Creek. This quiet valley offers camping and hiking opportunities, and supports one of the most diverse floras in the eastern Sierra Nevada. A Forest Service campground, information station, and wilderness trailhead are located at the roadend, elevation 9,200 feet. From Independence, Onion Valley Road climbs 5,000 feet into the Sierra, providing exceptional views of the Inyo Mountains, the cinder cones of the Big Pine-Taboose lava field, and 14,375-foot Mount Williamson, the second-tallest peak in California.

The Onion Valley area offers a unique opportunity to see seven different pine species growing within a few miles of one another. Five species can be seen at the roadend in Onion Valley. Foxtail, limber, lodgepole, and a few whitebark pines grow together in the campground; nearby, on the rocky slope traversed by the Kearsarge Pass Trail, stand some large Jeffrey pines. Pinyon pine becomes the dominant conifer a short distance below Onion Valley, and a stand of ponderosa pine—unusual in the Eastern Sierra—thrives at Seven Pines Grove, located where Onion Valley Road crosses Independence Creek about eight miles below the roadend.

Onion Valley is named for the wild swamp onion, *Allium validum*, whose

Onion Valley is known for its summer displays of mountain wildflowers. CARR CLIFTON

During the height of the mining activity on the peak, Kearsarge was the largest settlement in newly established Inyo County. For a time, it vied with Independence to become the county seat. Kearsarge was destroyed by an avalanche in 1867. Building foundations from its short-lived era are still visible at several spots along upper Onion Valley Road.

Historic Kearsarge Pass is a five-mile hike from Onion Valley. For centuries, the pass was used by Indians for trans-Sierra travel and trade. It was also a major crossing point for 19th-century explorers, miners, and mountaineers. William Brewer, who led California's first geological survey of the Sierra Nevada in 1864, described the setting at Kearsarge Pass as "one of sublime desolation." The 10-mile round-trip outing between Onion Valley and Kearsarge Pass makes a rigorous but rewarding day hike. From Onion Valley, the Kearsarge Trail heads west, enters the John Muir Wilderness, and crests the Sierra at the 11,823-foot pass. The celebrated view from Kearsarge Pass offers a panorama of glaciated Sierra peaks and lake basins in the John Muir Wilderness and Kings Canyon National Park.

• *In Independence, turn west off U.S. 395 onto Market St. (Onion Valley Road) for the 15-mile drive to* **Onion Valley***. Snow restricts travel during the winter, but in most years the way is clear by mid-May.*

rosy-pink flowers dot the moist, north slope of the canyon during July. Scores of other wildflowers bloom here in summer, including monkshood, tiger lily, corn lily, fireweed, angelica, shooting star, buckwheat, and paintbrush.

In 1864, woodcutters from Independence found gold and silver on the slopes of Kearsarge Peak, the prominent, triangular mountain due north of Onion Valley. By 1866, upper Independence Creek was the site of the busy mining camp of Kearsarge.

Above: Vista of the Sierra Nevada and Owens Valley from Mazourka Peak in the Inyo Mountains northeast of Independence. BILL EVARTS
Opposite: Folded and tilted layers of metamorphic rock form the walls of scenic Mazourka Canyon in the Inyo Mountains. BILL EVARTS

Inyo Mountains

The White-Inyo Range extends from the northern Mojave Desert into Nevada and is capped by the highest peaks of the Great Basin. South of Westgard Pass, the range is known as the Inyo Mountains and comprises some of the most rugged and remote territory in eastern California. *Inyo* is a Paiute word meaning "dwelling place of a great spirit."

Rising steeply from the desert floor and cresting near 11,000 feet, the Inyo Mountains parallel the Sierra Nevada for over 50 miles. This is a desert range and, unlike the Sierra, it has no glaciers, perennially snow-capped peaks, alpine lakes, or roaring streams. Instead, the Inyo Mountains offer a more subtle landscape and a different combination of attractions: isolated country, fascinating geology, desert wildflowers, fragrant pinyon-juniper woodlands, ancient bristlecone pines, and stunning vistas of the Sierra Nevada.

Mazourka Canyon Tour: Heading east from Independence, Mazourka Canyon Road provides the best access into the heart of the Inyo Mountains.

About three miles from town, the road dips where it crosses a fault scarp left by the powerful earthquake that leveled Lone Pine in 1872. The scarp's brushy slope can be traced both north and south for some distance.

Continuing east, Mazourka Canyon Road crosses the Owens River channel. Just before the pavement ends, the road passes the now-vacant site of Bend City, one of two sizable mining camps that existed on the western flank of the Inyo Mountains in the early 1860s. The site of Kearsarge Station, a depot on the abandoned Carson & Colorado Railroad, is located on the south side of the road here.

The Inyos' vivid, folded layers of metamorphic rock loom ahead as you resume driving toward the mouth of Mazourka Canyon. Rather than running east to west down the slope of the range, the canyon cuts an unusual north-south corridor. It extends deep into the Inyo Mountains, following a band of steeply tilted and faulted rock.

As you gain elevation, the flora makes a gradual transition from Mojave Desert species to Great Basin species; following wet winters, Mazourka Canyon is splashed with color from desert wildflowers common to both regions. In spring and early summer, visitors are likely to see the blooms of bush sunflower (or brittlebush), prince's plume, Mojave aster, and beavertail cactus.

Mazourka Canyon Road levels out at Badger Flat, a large sagebrush-covered bench surrounded by fragrant Utah juniper and single-leaf pinyon, the most widely distributed trees in the Great Basin. From Badger Flat (8,800 feet), a 1.5-mile hike (or bumpy drive) continues northwest to 9,941-foot Mazourka Peak (Barber Peak on some maps). The peak directly overlooks Owens Valley and Big Pine-Taboose lava field and offers a sweeping view of the Sierra's eastern escarpment. A 4-wheel drive road continues east from Badger Flat, ascending to a stand of western bristlecone pine near the crest of the mountains. Another 4-wheel-drive route heads north via Papoose Flat to rejoin the pavement at Eureka Valley Road.

• *Bring extra water and fill up with gas before starting the 40-mile round-trip drive up* **Mazourka Canyon** *to Badger Flat. Most of Mazourka Canyon Road is unpaved and high-clearance or 4-wheel-drive vehicles are recommended. Contact the Mount Whitney Ranger Station in Lone Pine for further information on travel in the* **Inyo Mountains**. *Mazourka Canyon Road leaves U.S. 395 on the southeast side of Independence.*

Winnedumah Paiute Monument

The best-known landmark of the Inyo Mountains is Winnedumah Paiute Monument. Winnedumah is an 80-foot granite spire, protruding like a thumb along the low section of the Inyo Mountain skyline east of Independence. According to Native American legend, Winnedumah was formed during a battle when a Shoshone Indian loosed an arrow across Owens Valley at two Paiute Indian brothers standing on the Inyo Mountains' crest. One Paiute was killed, and his brother—now the pillar—was turned to stone at the Shoshone's command, "Winnedumah!" or "Stay right where you are!"

• *Winnedumah Paiute Monument is easily discernible from vantage points in the Independence area. The spire is most visible in the light of dawn or early morning and again at dusk.*

Trout pond, Mt. Whitney Hatchery. BILL EVARTS

Mount Whitney State Fish Hatchery

Many people are surprised to learn that trout are not native to most of the eastern Sierra Nevada. Trout were probably first introduced to the Mono Basin from the Walker River drainage during the 1850s. During the 1870s, rainbow and golden trout were transplanted to Inyo County waters from streams in the western and southern regions of the Sierra. By the end of the 19th century, trout were well established in a number of Eastern Sierra drainages. The completion of the Mount Whitney State Fish Hatchery near Independence in 1917 marked the beginning of the region's highly acclaimed trout management program.

The hatchery has been an Eastern Sierra landmark for nearly 75 years. Surrounded by lawns and shade trees, the hatchery is a vine-covered, Tudor-style building with a tower at its south end. The structure's two-foot-thick walls are built of granite rocks and boulders that were collected on site and sorted—rather than cut—to fit together. This hatchery, the first of four in Inyo and Mono counties, was heralded as one of the world's largest fish-rearing facilities when it began operating in 1917.

Today, an estimated 20 million rainbow and 3 million brown and eastern brook trout eggs are incubated annually at Mount Whitney State Fish Hatchery. Shortly before hatching, most of these eggs are shipped to one of the other Eastern Sierra hatcheries where the fish are reared in outdoor ponds. Lakes in the Sierra backcountry are planted with fingerlings, young fish one to two inches long, that are dropped into the water from airplanes. Other trout remain in hatchery ponds to develop into 9- to 12-inch-long adults, and these are released into streams throughout the Eastern Sierra. The entire rearing process, from egg to catchable-size adult, requires 9 to 12 months.

Visitors can observe three species of broodstock—brown, eastern brook, and rainbow trout—in the hatchery's outdoor raceways and pond. Informative displays about California trout culture and management are mounted inside the building; incubators and tanks are off limits to the public. The hatchery's quiet grounds provide a pleasant setting for a picnic or a respite from travel. A Forest Service campground is located about one mile past the hatchery on Oak Creek. The creek is lined with black oak, *Quercus kellogii*, and also supports one of the few stands of interior live oak, *Quercus wislizneii*, on the east side of the Sierra.

• *Mount Whitney State Fish Hatchery* is open daily 8 a.m. to 5 p.m. Drive 2 miles north of Independence on U.S. 395, turn west on Fish Hatchery Road and continue 1 mile to the facility.

• *Other Eastern Sierra Hatcheries*: Black Rock State Fish Hatchery is located 8 miles north of Independence, just west of U.S. 395. Fish Springs State Fish Hatchery is 22 miles north of Independence, a short distance west of U.S. 395. Hot Creek State Fish Hatchery, the largest hatchery in the Eastern Sierra, is located about 1 mile east of U.S. 395 near the Mammoth/June Lakes Airport. All four hatcheries are open to the public and operated by the California Department of Fish and Game.

Tule Elk of Owens Valley

by David E. Babb

Tule elk near the Owens River. RALPH CLEVENGER

The tule elk, found only in California, is the smallest of the three subspecies of elk. An adult bull may weigh up to 550 pounds, several hundred pounds less than its Rocky Mountain cousin. The tule elk's coat is dark brown with a whitish rump patch. Males are distinguished by their heavily maned necks and majestic spreading antlers. During the mating season, a single mature bull takes charge of a herd of females and calves, fending off any challenge from other males. A bugling sound made by the bulls may precede a fierce fight for control of the harem.

Prior to the 19th century, an estimated 500,000 tule elk roamed California west of the Sierra Nevada; herds inhabited the bottomlands and foothills of the Central Valley, from Shasta County to Kern County, and ranged along the coast, from San Francisco to Ventura. By the 1870s tule elk had been forced to the brink of extinction by hunting and loss of habitat. In 1874, when many believed the species was extinct, a small number of tule elk were found on the San Joaquin Valley ranch of cattleman Henry Miller. Given protection on Miller's vast holdings, they began a remarkable comeback: 28 elk were counted in an 1895 census, and their numbers grew steadily thereafter.

The State of California gave the tule elk permanent protection and began to reintroduce them to areas where they previously flourished. One small group was released in Yosemite National Park in the early 1930s, but the National Park Service soon requested their removal. Lone Pine businessman G. Walter Dow

Tule elk bull and cow. JOHN D. WEHAUSEN

convinced the State to relocate the animals to Owens Valley. In 1933, 27 tule elk were shipped from Yosemite to Owens Valley; the following year, 27 elk from the Central Valley were added to the herd. Although not native to the Eastern Sierra, the tule elk thrived in Owens Valley and the herd grew rapidly.

Today there are six distinct herds between Owens Lake and the outskirts of Bishop, comprising about 500 animals. Statewide, the tule elk population now exceeds 2,500. In recent years, many of California's new tule elk herds have been established with individuals relocated from Owens Valley.

Where to see tule elk. Here are several locales where elk can be spotted: east side of Owens River near Manzanar-Reward Road, which intersects U.S. 395 five miles south of Independence; Tinemaha Reservoir Wildlife Overlook, on U.S. 395 seven miles south of Big Pine; along Warm Springs Road, from its intersection with U.S. 395 (two miles south of central Bishop) to the base of the White Mountains. During summer, tule elk bulls may be seen from roads and paths along both sides of the lower Owens River. (Please leave ranch gates as you find them.)

White Mountains/Big Pine Region

The White Mountains, a lofty barren chain vying with the Sierras in altitude, rose in splendid rank and stretched southeast parallel with the great range. Down the broad intermediate trough flows Owens River, alternately through expanses of natural meadow and desolate reaches of sage.

The Sierra, as we travelled southward, grew bolder and bolder, strong granite spurs plunging steeply down into the desert.... The mountain forms and mode of sculpture of the opposite ranges are altogether different. The White and Inyo chains, formed chiefly of uplifted sedimentary beds, are largely covered with soil, and wherever the solid rock is exposed, its easily traced strata plains and soft wooded surface combined in producing a general aspect of breadth and smoothness; while the Sierra, here more than anywhere else, hold up a front of solid stone, carved into most intricate and highly ornamental forms.

—Clarence King,
Mountaineering in the Sierra Nevada, 1872

White Mountains
Sidebar: Bighorn Sheep
in the Eastern Sierra
Big Pine Canyon

Left: Mountain chickadee, a widespread resident of woodlands and forests in the White-Inyo Range. B. "MOOSE" PETERSON
Opposite: Dawn light at the Patriarch Grove in the White Mountains' Ancient Bristlecone Pine Forest. LARRY ULRICH

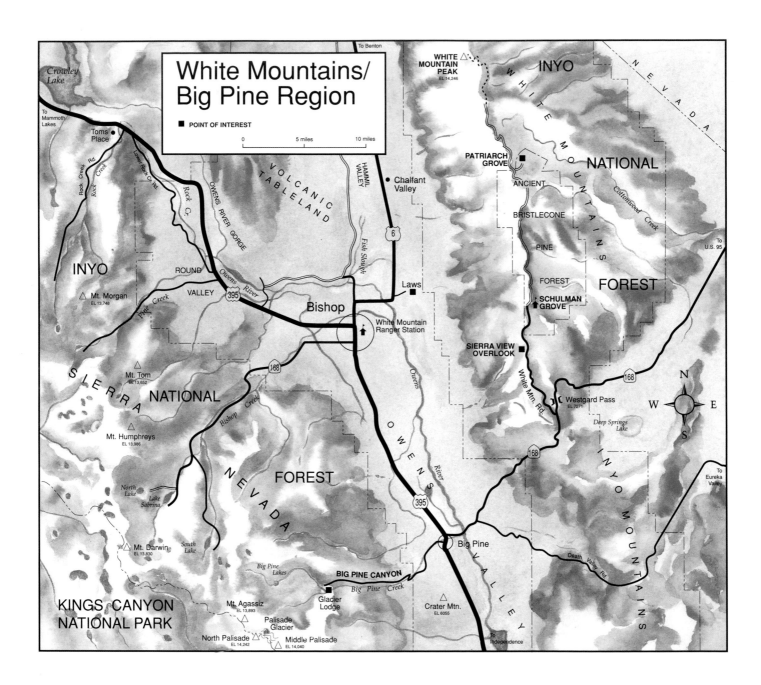

White Mountains/ Big Pine Region

■ POINT OF INTEREST

0   5 miles   10 miles

Crowley Lake

To Benton

To Mammoth Lakes

Toms Place

INYO

Mt. Morgan
EL 13,748

Rock Creek Rd.
Lower Rock Cr. Rd.
Rock Cr.
Rock Creek

OWENS RIVER GORGE

VOLCANIC TABLELAND

HAMMIL VALLEY

Chalfant Valley

6

WHITE MOUNTAIN PEAK
EL 14,246

INYO

NATIONAL

PATRIARCH GROVE

ANCIENT

BRISTLECONE

PINE

FOREST

SCHULMAN GROVE

Cottonwood Creek

To U.S. 95

NATIONAL

FOREST

ROUND

VALLEY

Pryor Creek

Owens River

395

Fish Slough

Laws

Bishop

White Mountain Ranger Station

SIERRA

Mt. Tom
EL 13,652

NATIONAL

168

Bishop Creek

Mt. Humphreys
EL 13,986

NEVADA

FOREST

North Lake
Lake Sabrina

Mt. Darwin
EL 13,830

South Lake

Owens River

SIERRA VIEW OVERLOOK

White Mtn. Rd.

Westgard Pass
EL 7271

168

Deep Springs Lake

168

N
W   E
S

INYO

To Eureka Valley

Big Pine Lakes

BIG PINE CANYON

Big Pine Creek

Glacier Lodge

395

Big Pine

Death Valley Rd.

MOUNTAINS

Mt. Agassiz
EL 13,893

Palisade Glacier

North Palisade
EL 14,242

Middle Palisade
EL 14,040

KINGS CANYON NATIONAL PARK

Crater Mtn.
EL 6055

VALLEY

To Independence

NEVADA

White Mountains

The White and Inyo mountains parallel the Sierra and form the highest range of the Great Basin. The northern part of the range is known as the White Mountains and extends about 50 miles from Westgard Pass (east of Big Pine) northward into Nevada. Among California mountain ranges, only the Sierra Nevada is taller. The White Mountains claim California's third-highest mountain, White Mountain Peak (14,246 feet), as well as Nevada's tallest point, Boundary Peak (13,140 feet).

Situated in the rain shadow of the Sierra Nevada, most areas of the White Mountains receive only 5 to 14 inches of precipitation a year. From a distance the range appears stark, arid, and inhospitable, yet thriving in this harsh environment—subjected to the extremes of both drought and cold—are groves of some of the earth's most extraordinary and long-lived trees: western bristlecone pine. The oldest known continuously growing organism in the world is found in the White Mountains—a 4,700-year-old bristlecone pine named Methuselah.

Although the White Mountains and the Sierra Nevada reached their tremendous height due to simultaneous mountain-building processes, the two ranges are geologically distinct. The White Mountains are composed primarily of 500- to 600-million-year-old sedimentary formations and contain some of the oldest rock in California. The Sierra is largely formed of granite. The only areas of the White Mountains that resemble the Sierra are its northernmost summits, Boundary and Montgomery peaks, which are composed of 100- to 150-million-year-old granite.

Despite the rigors of the White Mountains' environment, over 1,000 plant species have been identified in the range. During late spring, the blooms of prickly poppy, apricot mallow, penstemon, phlox, and other desert flowers sprinkle the lower slopes. Above treeline, the subalpine and alpine vegetation comprises a variety of extremely hardy tundra-type plants. August is the best month to see wildflowers at the higher elevations, including onion-flowered buckwheat, ground rose (also in the buckwheat family), alpine meadow-rue, and Mono clover.

In addition to their diverse flora, the White Mountains support many forms of wildlife. Mountain bluebirds, mountain chickadees, Clark's nut-crackers, juncos, and nuthatches frequent wooded areas; white-throated swifts, hawks, and golden eagles soar along the ridges. The range is also

Above: Western bristlecone pines often live for 2,000 years or more. WILLIAM NEILL
Opposite: In contrast to the granitic Sierra, the White Mountains are primarily composed of sedimentary rock. WILLIAM NEILL

home to deer, bighorn sheep, mountain lion, bobcat, coyote, and wild horses.

The most intriguing resident of the White Mountains is the western bristlecone pine, *Pinus longaeva*. The Ancient Bristlecone Pine Forest, a 58,000-acre reserve established for research and public enjoyment in 1958, protects the majority of the range's bristlecones. Although the western bristlecone grows in Utah and Nevada, the White Mountains claim the oldest living specimens and most extensive stands of this astonishing conifer. A related species, *Pinus aristata*, grows in Colorado, New Mexico, and Arizona.

Visitors to the Ancient Bristlecone Pine Forest would probably agree with John Muir, who described the trees as "irrepressibly and extravagantly picturesque." Bristlecones are not lofty beauties; few grow taller than 30 feet. Instead, they enchant us with their stout, gnarled trunks, knotted limbs, and golden-hued wood. Clinging to steep, dry, rocky slopes, the trees are impressive models of economy, stamina, and tenacity. Bristlecones grow very slowly, often less than an inch in diameter per 100 years. Sculpted over centuries by wind, blowing ice and sand, and occasionally fire, many bristlecones develop unique and exquisite shapes.

The bristlecone pine exhibits a variety of adaptations that allow it to survive, and even to thrive, in such a severe environment. Unable to tolerate competition from many other plants, it does best in the White Mountains' arid, alkaline, dolomitic soils where there is a paucity of competing plant species. The tree's shallow root system is also well suited to this nutrient-poor mountain soil. It favors slow growth, a necessary component in the bristlecone's longevity.

Where growing conditions are most restrictive and adverse, bristlecones tend to live longer. Bristlecones that are more "deprived" of available moisture and nutrients produce wood that is more dense and resinous, and therefore more resistant to disease, fungi, and insects. Specimens located on exposed, dry slopes usually survive more than 2,000 years, while those in more protected areas live an average of 1,200 years. Even after most of a bristlecone pine is dead, a portion of it may continue to grow, deriving sustenance from a mere strip of living tissue. The wood of dead trees remains intact for thousands of years because of a compact cell structure preserved with abundant resin.

The bristlecone pine can easily be distinguished from its neighbor, the limber pine, *Pinus flexilis*. The bristlecone's deep green needles, which can live for over 35 years, are less than two inches long and uni-formly cover ends of the branches in a bottle-brush configuration for a foot or more; limber pine needles, also grouped in fives, are slightly longer and appear in tufts at the branch tips. Bristlecone's immature cones usually have a deep purple hue (about 25% of the trees have light green cones), while mature cones are brownish and exhibit a distinctive, curved bristle on each scale. The cones of limber pines lack the telltale bristle. Virtually all the trees at the Schulman Grove Visitor Center are bristlecone pines; limber pines grow along the roadside just south of the grove entrance and farther north within the Ancient Bristlecone Pine Forest.

Above: Western bristlecone pine. GORDON WILTSIE
Opposite: The oldest continuously living organism is a bristlecone pine. LARRY ULRICH

Since the late 1950s, when Dr. Edmund Schulman discovered the great age of some bristlecone pines, the species has been recognized as a valuable asset to scientific research. Tree rings accurately reflect yearly precipitation and summer tempera-tures. Counting and examining the rings of dead bristlecone pines—as well as examining their living tissue—has enabled scientists to construct a continuous climatic record spanning over 9,000 years. Most of this research has been conducted at the University of Arizona's tree research labs in Tucson. The University of California White Mountain Research Station maintains three laboratories north of Schulman Grove; its activities include ongoing study of the bristlecone pine as well as research in high-altitude physiology, botany, biology, geology, and climatology.

The scenic drive from Owens Valley to the Ancient Bristlecone Pine Forest is a 25-mile, 6,000-foot climb that passes through at least four major plant communities. The journey begins in shadscale scrub, enters pinyon-juniper woodland between 6,500 and 9,000 feet, crosses through a band of Great Basin montane scrub, and arrives in the bristlecone pine forest near 9,500 feet. The alpine fell-field community is encountered above timberline (about 11,500 feet) and is home to a variety of hardy, low-growing herbaceous plants.

The first leg of the trip follows Highway 168, which crosses the White-Inyo Range at 7,271-foot Westgard Pass. Once known as the Deep Springs Valley Toll Road, this stretch of the highway was first built to serve mines and ranches east of the White Mountains. Tolls were collected from 1873 until 1916, making it the last toll road in California. The following destinations are reached by taking White Mountain Road, which heads north from Highway 168 about 1.5 miles west of Westgard Pass.

Sierra View Overlook: Located at 9,000 feet in the White Mountains' pinyon-juniper belt, this overlook offers breathtaking panoramas of the Eastern Sierra and has a display that identifies the major peaks and mountain ranges in view. A short trail traverses a hillock to an unobstructed view of the Sierra that takes in 100 miles of the range, including California's two tallest peaks, Mount Whitney and Mount Williamson. To the south lie the Inyo Mountains, their rounded contours a sharp contrast to the jagged Sierra Nevada.

Schulman Grove: Schulman Grove (10,100 feet) is located at the southern end of the Ancient Bristlecone Pine Forest and is home to the oldest known bristlecone pines in the world.

A visitor center and picnic area are located near the grove's entrance. During summer months, Forest Service ranger naturalists give lively interpretive talks at the visitor center.

The grove has two self-guided trails, both supplied with pamphlets that interpret features along the way. The mile-long Discovery Trail winds through a stand of gnarled ancients that includes Pine Alpha, the first tree over 4,000 years old discovered by Dr. Schulman. From the trail you can see the abrupt line where pale dolomitic soil, inhabited by bristlecone pine, adjoins richer sandstone soil dominated by sagebrush. The Methuselah Trail is a 4.5-mile loop that leads to the "Forest of the Ancients," site of 4,700-year-old Methuselah. Pine Alpha and Methuselah are unmarked, so their anonymity protects them from vandalism.

Patriarch Grove: Some of the most picturesque bristlecone pines are found at Patriarch Grove (11,000 feet), located just below timberline at the northern edge of the Ancient Bristlecone Pine Forest. Among them is the Patriarch, a tree whose circumference of 36 feet, 8 inches makes it the largest known bristlecone pine. Like many bristlecones at this elevation, the 1,500-year-old Patriarch is weather-worn and twisted, growing low to the ground with multiple trunks. As you walk the footpaths,

notice the difference in the vegetation as compared to Schulman Grove; instead of sagebrush scrub, most understory plants at Patriarch Grove are low-growing alpine species, well adapted to this area's short summers and long, severe winters.

White Mountain Peak: As with Mount Whitney, the ascent of White Mountain Peak (14,246 feet) is not a technical climb, but the 15-mile round trip with a 2,600-foot elevation gain makes for a strenuous hike. Camping is permitted near the trailhead (fire permits required for stoves), and individuals planning to climb White Mountain may find it convenient to stay overnight here. Hikers should bring generous amounts of water, sunscreen, and warm clothing.

• *Allow at least half a day for a trip to Schulman Grove and a full day for a visit to Patriarch Grove. It is 35 miles one way from Big Pine to the Patriarch Grove and much of the road is slow and winding.*

Begin the trip to the **White Mountains** *on Highway 168, which heads east from U.S. 395 just north of Big Pine. Drive 13 miles east to Cedar Flat, then turn north onto White Mountain Road. From here it is 8 miles to* **Sierra View Overlook** *and 10 miles to* **Schulman Grove,** *where the pavement ends. A dirt road, not highly recommended for low-clearance vehicles, automatic transmissions, RVs, or trailers, leads 11 miles to*

Patriarch Grove. Beyond the Patriarch Grove turnoff, the road continues 4.6 miles to the locked gate at the trailhead (11,650 feet) for hiking to **White Mountain Peak.** *The only campground near the Ancient Bristlecone Pine Forest is Grandview Campground, located about 5 miles north of Cedar Flat. Group camping is available near Cedar Flat by reservation; contact the White Mountain Ranger Station in Bishop. There is no gas, water, or food available in the White Mountains, so come fully prepared, even if just for a day. White Mountain Road is normally open from late May through November, depending on snowfall.*

Above: Ski-touring past a western bristlecone pine in the White Mountains. JIM STIMSON
Opposite: Looking west to the Sierra from the White Mountains' Sierra View Overlook. PAT O'HARA

Bighorn Sheep in the Eastern Sierra

by John D. Wehausen

Bighorn sheep inhabit the steep, rugged alpine country of the Sierra Nevada and White-Inyo Range. GALEN ROWELL / MOUNTAIN LIGHT

The bighorn sheep, one of California's most magnificent mammals, inhabits rugged, isolated areas in the Sierra Nevada and White-Inyo Range. It is renowned for its agility in negotiating the steep, rocky terrain that characterizes much of its habitat. The bighorn is the size of a deer, with a gray to brown pelage (coat), and a distinctive white rump patch. While the horns of the female are slender and erect with a slight curve, the impressive horns of the male grow outward, backward, and then forward in a spiral that can reach a complete circle in older rams. Adult rams travel in separate bands from the ewes and lambs during much of the year, joining them in the fall mating season when the rams exhibit their famous horn-clashing jousting matches.

Indians in the Eastern Sierra knew the habits of the bighorn sheep well, as evidenced by the rock blinds and projectile points they left behind in remote locations where only sheep would have been their prey. Centuries of hunting by Native Americans had little impact on bighorn sheep populations, but after the area was settled by whites in the late 19th century, the number of bighorn sheep began to steadily decline. By the turn of the century hundreds of thousands of domestic sheep grazed annually in Owens Valley, Mono Basin, and the surrounding mountains. They impinged on the habitat of the bighorn and brought in diseases, notably scabies and pneumonia, which spread among the native sheep and eventually decimated their populations.

Today, native bighorn populations remain in only four locations in the Eastern Sierra: the Mount Williamson area south of Independence, the area north of Independence from Kearsarge Pass to Taboose Pass, the north end of the White Mountains, and the east side of the Inyo Mountains. Since 1979, the California Department of Fish and Game and other public agencies have been working to increase the numbers of bighorn sheep in the Eastern Sierra; they have reintroduced bighorn sheep to three new areas of the Sierra and to Silver Canyon in the White Mountains. The total bighorn sheep population in the Sierra is currently about 325, while the total population in the White and Inyo mountains is about 250. The State of California has classified Sierra bighorn as a threatened species.

Where to see bighorn sheep.
Bighorn sheep are hard to spot, but it is a thrill to see them. In the Sierra, backpackers regularly report viewing sheep around Baxter Pass and the Rae Lakes. Rams are sometimes observed on the rocky slopes around Little Lakes Valley near the headwaters of Rock Creek, an area accessible as a day hike. Bighorn are also spotted above the Tioga Pass Road (Highway 120) in Lee Vining Canyon. In the White Mountains, they have been sighted to the west of White Mountain Road, about four miles north of Schulman Grove.

Big Pine Canyon

Big Pine Canyon is a quiet mountain retreat offering a wide range of attractions to Eastern Sierra visitors A creekside campground, picnic area, pack station, and resort are tucked between the canyon's steep walls and shaded by lofty Jeffrey pines. Big Pine Creek offers excellent trout fishing, and the canyon's trails provide access to backcountry lakes, the Sierra Nevada's largest glacier, and some of the most challenging alpine climbing areas in California.

Big Pine Canyon is one of the best places to observe the Eastern Sierra's glacial features. The scenic, 10-mile road that follows Big Pine Creek up the canyon traverses several large lateral moraines (ridges of dirt, gravel, and rock deposited by glaciers) and ends at the foot of a U-shaped, glacial valley. Middle Palisade Glacier can be spotted from the parking area near Glacier Lodge. This glacier is part of the Palisade group, the southernmost active glaciers in North America. The largest glacier in the Sierra Nevada, Palisade Glacier, is reached by hiking nine miles from the roadend in Big Pine Canyon.

The town of Big Pine, the canyon, and the creek were named for the extensive stands of Jeffrey pine found in this drainage. Jeffrey pines were an important source of wood for pioneers in the lightly-forested Eastern Sierra, and many stands were depleted in the 19th century. The Bell sawmill, one of the first in Inyo County, was built near lower Big Pine Creek in 1864.

At the turn of the century, upper Big Pine Canyon and the Big Pine Lakes were popular family retreats for Owens Valley residents. By the 1920s and 1930s, the canyon contained a small resort colony, attracting tourists year-round. The North Fork Trail, which leads to Big Pine Lakes, passes a stone cabin built by Hollywood star Lon Chaney in 1925. A moderate to strenuous day hike leads to Third Lake, where the water is milky-turquoise from glacial flour (pulverized rock) that flows into the lake from Palisade Glacier. Third Lake is about 10 miles round trip from the day-use parking area or 11 miles from the overnight "hiker" parking area.

• *Big Pine Canyon is open year-round to vehicle traffic. Take Glacier Lodge Road, named Crocker St. in downtown Big Pine, 10 miles west from U.S. 395 to the roadend at 7,800 feet. The Palisade glaciers are also visible from U.S. 395 just north of Big Pine and from Highway 168, east of town.*

Big Pine Canyon near Glacier Lodge, looking west toward Middle Palisade Glacier. BILL EVARTS

Bishop Region

The Sierra Nevada catches all the rains and clouds from the west — to the east are deserts — so, of course, this valley sees but little rain, but where streams come down from the Sierra they spread out and great meadows of green grass occur. Tens of thousands of the starving cattle of the state have been driven in here this year, and there is feed for twice as many more. Yet these meadows comprise not over one-tenth of the valley — the rest is desert.

— William H. Brewer,
Up and Down California in 1860-1864, 1864

Left: Western tanager, a colorful summer visitor to Eastern Sierra forests. JIM STROUP
Opposite: Quaking aspens and lodgepole pine, Bishop Creek Canyon. WILLIAM NEILL

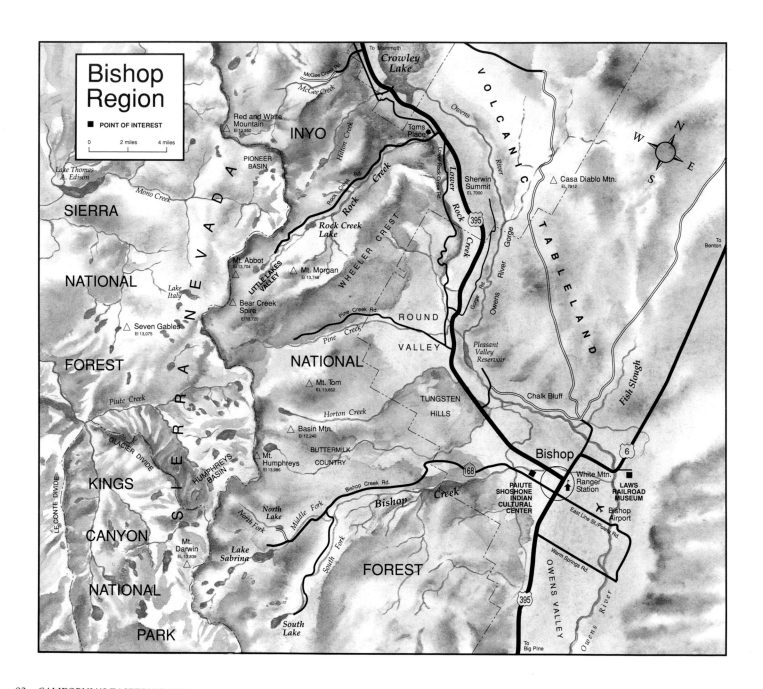

Bishop Region

■ POINT OF INTEREST

0   2 miles   4 miles

SIERRA

INYO

Crowley Lake

To Mammoth

McGee Creek Rd.

McGee Creek

Red and White Mountain
El 12,850

PIONEER BASIN

Lake Thomas A. Edison

Mono Creek

NATIONAL

Toms Place

Owens River

VOLCANIC

Casa Diablo Mtn.
El 7912

To Benton

Hilton Creek

Rock Creek Rd.

Rock Creek

Rock Creek Lake

Sherwin Summit
EL 7000

Lower Rock Creek Rd.

Lower Rock Creek

395

Owens River Gorge

TABLELAND

Mt. Abbot
El 13,704

LITTLE LAKES VALLEY

Mt. Morgan
El 13,748

WHEELER CREST

Lake Italy

Bear Creek Spire
El 13,720

Gorge Rd.

FOREST

Seven Gables
El 13,075

Pine Creek Rd.

Pine Creek

ROUND

VALLEY

Pleasant Valley Reservoir

Piute Creek

NATIONAL

Mt. Tom
EL 13,652

Horton Creek

TUNGSTEN HILLS

Fish Slough

Chalk Bluff

GLACIER DIVIDE

Basin Mtn.
El 12,240

BUTTERMILK COUNTRY

HUMPHREYS BASIN

KINGS

Mt. Humphreys
El 13,986

Bishop

168

White Mtn. Ranger Station

6

LAWS RAILROAD MUSEUM

LE CONTE DIVIDE

CANYON

North Lake

North Fork

Middle Fork

Bishop Creek Rd.

Bishop   Creek

PAIUTE SHOSHONE INDIAN CULTURAL CENTER

Bishop Airport

East Line St./Poleta Rd.

Mt. Darwin
El 13,839

Lake Sabrina

South Fork

FOREST

NATIONAL

South Lake

Warm Springs Rd.

OWENS VALLEY

Owens River

PARK

395

To Big Pine

To Big Pine

SIERRA NEVADA

Paiute Shoshone Indian Cultural Center

Paiute and Shoshone people have lived in the Eastern Sierra for centuries. Although hundreds of Owens Valley Paiutes were forced off their ancestral lands in the 1860s, many eventually returned and settled in the area. To become acquainted with the Eastern Sierra's rich Native American heritage, visit the Paiute Shoshone Indian Cultural Center. The Cultural Center is on the Bishop Reservation, one of four Indian reservations in Owens Valley. Located a short distance west of downtown Bishop, the Cultural Center houses a museum with excellent interpretive exhibits, an information desk, and a gift shop.

The largest exhibit in the Cultural Center's museum recreates a winter scene of a Paiute camp on Bishop Creek. Another exhibit depicts a *wogani* (pine nut camp house) and shows how *tuva* (pinyon pine nuts, a dietary staple) were gathered and prepared. Also replicated in the museum are a *toni*, the traditional Paiute willow and reed shelter, and a *musa*, the Paiute sweat house. The museum displays beautiful examples of Paiute basketry, beadwork, clothing, and traditional household items.

• **The Paiute Shoshone Cultural Center** *is 1 mile west of U.S. 395 on West Line St. in Bishop. It is open daily year-round, except for major holidays.*

Bishop Creek

The north, middle, and south forks of Bishop Creek tumble out of the high country, merge, and plummet 6,000 feet down a tremendous glacial canyon to the Owens Valley floor. Together they form one of the largest watersheds in the eastern Sierra Nevada. Imposing peaks marbled with rusty-red metamorphic rock rim the headwaters of Bishop Creek, adding a dramatic visual backdrop to a drainage renowned for trout fishing, summer wildflowers, and fall color. More than 80 backcountry lakes are located within a few miles of Bishop Creek trailheads. Lake Sabrina and South Lake, situated near the head of Bishop Creek's middle and south forks, are popular with anglers; nearby resorts offer boat and cabin rentals. Small, picturesque North Lake is located on the north fork of Bishop Creek.

Both the creek and the town of Bishop were named for Samuel A. Bishop, who established one of the original Owens Valley cattle ranches along lower Bishop Creek in 1861. When he arrived, the area was inhabited by Paiutes. The Indians lived near the creek, and during summer months, diverted its water to irrigate fields of taboose, *Cyperus esculentus*. Also known as yellow nut grass, the wild vegetable was cultivated for its edible, nut-like tubers.

During the early 1860s, friction between Indians and settlers erupted

Top: Bead-covered baskets and bead collar made by Owens Valley Paiutes. BILL EVARTS
Bottom: Cottonwoods growing along the bank of an irrigation ditch near Bishop. BILL EVARTS

Lake Sabrina, near the headwaters of the Middle Fork of Bishop Creek. GORDON WILTSIE

into armed conflict. One such incident, the Bishop Creek "Battle of the Ditch," occurred in April 1862. A party of 50 settlers attacked a band of Paiutes and soon discovered they were greatly outnumbered; the whites took cover in a Paiute irrigation ditch and eventually retreated.

By the 1870s, tension between white settlers and Paiutes had decreased and Bishop Creek was harnessed to drive the wheels of a water-powered grist mill. By 1905, Bishop Creek hydroelectric generators were supplying power to the western Nevada mining towns of Tonopah and Goldfield, 100 miles away. Locally, the Cardinal Mine began operations in

1906 on the middle fork of Bishop Creek and was touted as the "World's Greatest Gold Mine." In the beginning, output from the mine was modest, returning only $50,000 during its first 10 years. Reworking the claim in the 1930s, however, yielded $1.5 million in gold. But today, the "gold" of Bishop Creek is derived from its water and hydroelectric power; runoff from this watershed fills three reservoirs and fuels five powerhouses before entering the Los Angeles Aqueduct.

South Lake: Set in a glacial basin and surrounded by jagged peaks and ridges, South Lake (9,755 feet) is the highest and largest reservoir in the

Bishop Creek drainage. A popular trail into the backcountry leads 5.5 miles from South Lake over Bishop Pass (11,972 feet) and descends through Dusy Basin to connect with the John Muir Trail. Other wilderness trails originate in South Lake Basin, providing access to a number of backcountry lakes. Stands of aspen and willow flourish in lower Bishop Creek canyon, producing brilliant displays of autumn color. A resort in the canyon offers year-round lodging and winter access to cross-country ski trails.

Lake Sabrina: Located on the middle fork of Bishop Creek, Lake Sabrina (9,132 feet) is ringed with majestic 13,000-foot granite peaks. Small glaciers are evident on the basin's upper rock faces, reminders of the vast sheets of ice that scoured these steep canyon walls and quarried out U-shaped valleys during the Pleistocene ice ages. Trails lead from Sabrina Basin to dozens of backcountry lakes, but none cross the Sierra crest here because the terrain is too rugged and steep.

North Lake: Dramatic red cliffs rim North Lake (9,200 feet), a shallow, reed-dotted lake that is slowly becoming a meadow. There is good lake fishing here, and pleasant hiking trails wind through adjacent woodlands and meadows. From the campground at North Lake, an 11-

mile trail heads west over Piute Pass (11,423 feet), descending into spectacular Humphreys Basin in the John Muir Wilderness. A second campground trailhead marks the way to Lamarck Lakes (four miles); the lower portion of this trail offers an easy mile-long climb to Grass Lake (9,900 feet).

• *Reach **Bishop Creek Canyon** by taking West Line St. (Highway 168) west from downtown Bishop. The road passes the California State Historic Landmark for the "Battle of the Ditch" after 5.3 miles. Turn left at a marked junction 15 miles from Bishop and continue 6 miles to reach **South Lake**. To reach **Lake Sabrina**, go straight ahead at this junction and continue 4 miles to the roadend. Ruins of the Cardinal Mine are visible from Highway 168, just east of the residential area of Aspendell. The turnoff to **North Lake** is located 1 mile before Lake Sabrina. Steep, narrow, and partially paved, the 2-mile road to North Lake is not recommended for RVs or trailers.*

Laws Museum / Carson & Colorado Railroad

The last narrow-gauge railroad to serve as a common carrier west of the Rocky Mountains operated in Owens Valley. Named the Carson & Colorado, and known affectionately as the "Slim Princess," the railroad trans-ported freight and passengers in Owens Valley until 1960. Today, the Laws Railroad Museum and Historical Site near Bishop preserves the legacy of this rail line, which conducted business here for 77 years. The museum grounds contain the original Laws Depot, Laws Post Office, and Agent's House, as well as a locomotive, a string of cars, and exhibits of railroad memorabilia. Visitors may tour the train and museum buildings, which house fascinating collections from Owens Valley pioneer days.

The Carson & Colorado was built to serve the mining towns of western Nevada and eastern California, and plans were made to extend it to the Mojave Desert. Construction began near Carson City, Nevada in 1880. The line was completed as far south as Benton, California in 1882, and reached Owens Valley the following year. When it was complete, the Carson & Colorado covered 300 miles. It ran south from Moundhouse, Nevada, crossed 7,132-foot Montgomery Pass, passed through Laws, and headed down Owens Valley to its terminus at Keeler on the east shore of Owens Lake.

The depot at Laws, originally called Bishop Station, was constructed in 1883, and the community of Laws soon grew up around it. The railroad provided an important transportation link between the Eastern Sierra and distant towns and cities of western

Top: Railroad crossing sign, Laws. JEFF BROUWS
Bottom: Visitors to Laws can climb aboard a train that once carried passengers on the Carson & Colorado Railroad. JOHN EVARTS

Nevada and northern California. Owens Valley ranchers and farmers prospered as the Carson & Colorado Railroad opened up new markets—some as far away as San Francisco—for their livestock and produce.

Passenger service north of Laws ended in 1932, but Southern Pacific, which bought the line in 1900, operated it between Laws and Keeler until 1960. After the final run, Southern Pacific donated Engine No. 9, a string of cars, and the Laws Depot to the City of Bishop and the County of Inyo.

Owens Valley's second railroad, the now-abandoned standard-gauge "Jawbone Branch" of the Southern Pacific, was built to haul equipment and supplies during construction of the Los Angeles Aqueduct. The line extended from Mojave to Owenyo (a Carson & Colorado depot northeast of Lone Pine) and provided passenger service until 1934. Its rails are still visible along the west side of Owens Lake.

• Laws Railroad Museum is 4 miles north of Bishop on U.S. Highway 6. A right turn on Silver Canyon Road leads to the museum, which is open daily from 10 a.m. to 4 p.m. The museum's reception center offers a comprehensive selection of books and gifts, with a special emphasis on railroads. Admission is free.

The Carson & Colorado depot is still standing in the town of Keeler, a short drive off Highway 136. The Lone Pine station of the Jawbone Branch is located northeast of Lone Pine, 1.7 miles east of U.S. 395 on Lone Pine Narrow Gauge Road. Carson & Colorado locomotive #18 is displayed in Dehy Park in Independence.

Owens River

The Owens River drains the entire eastern Sierra Nevada watershed south of the Mono Lake Basin. Like other rivers of the Great Basin, it flows into a desert sink rather than running out to sea. Called "Wakopee" by the Paiutes, the 120-mile river rises at the head of Long Valley northeast of Mammoth, meanders through Long and Owens valleys, and disappears in the vast playa of Owens Lake south of Lone Pine.

The City of Los Angeles has diverted water from the Owens River drainage since 1913. As owner of most of the land bordering the river, the city allows access to its property for day-use recreation. Renowned for fishing, the Owens River also attracts visitors who come to stroll along its quiet banks, watch for wildlife among its riparian thickets, or cool off in its water on hot summer days.

During the Pleistocene—which ended about 10,000 years ago—an ice-age "Owens River" spilled out of Mono Basin, flowed into ancient Owens Lake, and extended far beyond the Eastern Sierra. At various times the

Owens River near Bishop. BILL EVARTS

river connected a chain of lakes that occupied the present-day desert basins of China Lake, Searles Lake, Panamint Valley, and Death Valley. Several destinations featured in this book, including Mono Lake, Owens River Gorge, Owens Lake, and Fossil Falls, are remnants of this vast drainage.

Near its headwaters, Owens River meanders through Long Valley's grassy meadows. This beautiful stretch of river is known for superb fly-fishing, but anglers should be aware that private property limits river access in some areas here. The Owens River campground at Benton Crossing offers the best river access in Long Valley. At the southern end of the valley, the river is impounded in Crowley Lake Reservoir, one of California's premier trout-fishing lakes.

The Owens River Gorge, 16 miles in length, begins just south of Crowley Lake. The ice-age predecessor of Owens River carved this 700-foot chasm through the porous rock of the Volcanic Tableland. The gorge's sheer walls provide nesting sites for eagles and other birds of prey. Beginning in the early 1950s, Owens River water was rerouted past the lower gorge through tunnels and turbines to generate hydro-electric power. In an effort to restore the lower gorge's famous trout fishery, a modest flow was re-established in 1991. Pleasant Valley Reservoir and a campground are situated at the mouth of the gorge.

Bordered by willow, cattail, rushes, and cottonwood, the river cuts a winding green path along Owens Valley's desert floor. From Pleasant Valley Reservoir, the river flows east, skirting the base of 200-foot-high Chalk Bluff. The bluff derives its name not from chalk, but from the white pumice that is exposed here at the base of the Volcanic Tableland. Beyond Chalk Bluff, the river swings south and passes to the east of Bishop, this stretch is popular for canoeing and innertubing.

Although the aqueduct intake south of Big Pine greatly reduces its water volume, the lower Owens River still supports a variety of wildlife. Tule elk and beaver inhabit the riparian corridor; large-mouth bass, catfish, and bluegill thrive in the sluggish warm water; and numerous species of birds flock along the river banks.

Year-round fishing is permitted on Owens River below Crowley Lake. Much of the land owned by the City of Los Angeles is leased for cattle grazing, so please close any gates you open when driving across this property.

• A selection of routes that provide access to the **Owens River** is listed below. With the exception of Highway 6, all of the roads listed head east from U.S. 395.

Mammoth Area:
• Benton Crossing Road, 10 miles north of Tom's Place or 5 miles south of Mammoth Junction
Bishop Area:
• Gorge Road, 12 miles north of Bishop. Turn north (left) at the "T" intersection 0.7 miles after leaving U.S. 395; right

A lush riparian corridor along the lower Owens River east of Big Pine. BILL EVARTS

turns at 3 and 6 miles past the "T" lead to overlooks of the gorge
• *Pleasant Valley/Chalk Bluff Road, 6 miles north of Bishop*
• *U.S. Highway 6 (north from Bishop); go 1.5 miles on Highway 6, then turn north onto Five Bridges Road. After crossing the river, Five Bridges Road continues north and swings west to intersect with Chalk Bluff Road, which runs along the north side of the river*
• *East Line St., downtown Bishop*
• *Warm Springs Road, 2 miles south of Bishop*

Big Pine Area:
• *Highway 168 east, just north of Big Pine*
• *Aberdeen Station Road, 10 miles south of Big Pine*

Independence Area:
• *Manzanar-Reward Road, 1/4 mile north of the historic marker at Manzanar*

Lone Pine Area:
• *Lone Pine Narrow Gauge Road, 1 mile north of Lone Pine*
• *Highway 136, just south of Lone Pine*

Trout fishing on upper Owens River. TONY HERTZ

The Volcanic Tableland is cut by the 700-foot-deep Owens River Gorge. BILL EVARTS

Fish Slough / Volcanic Tableland

Hidden in the desert north of Bishop is a unique and intriguing environment—the oasis of Fish Slough. A remarkable sight in this arid region, the lush wetlands of Fish Slough cover hundreds of acres and contain about a dozen ponds. Fish Slough is fed by the last remaining natural springs on the Owens Valley floor and represents a habitat that has all but vanished from the region. An outing to this area can be coupled with an excursion into the rugged Volcanic Tableland.

The Volcanic Tableland is a broad, rolling plateau that rises near Crowley Lake and slopes nearly 3,000 feet down to Owens Valley. The springs of Fish Slough surface along the tableland's southeastern edge and owe their existence to this unusual geologic formation. The tableland was formed about 700,000 years ago when the colossal Long Valley volcanic eruption blanketed the region with a deep layer of scorching hot ash and rock. The volcanic ash fused into a porous, pink-and-beige rock known as Bishop tuff. The tuff, which is hundreds of feet thick, acts as a reservoir; it captures runoff that flows through the porous rock and eventually resurfaces at Fish Slough.

Fish Slough: Paiute Indians inhabited the Fish Slough area when pioneers first arrived in Owens Valley during the 1860s. They skillfully utilized the wetland's abundance of food resources, including Indian rice grass (*Oryzopsis hymenoides*), a wild grain they harvested with the aid of large, flat baskets. Fish Slough's ponds and marshes provided the Indians with fish and mollusks, while waterfowl and other wildlife attracted to the springs were a source of game. Visitors to Fish Slough may see evidence of the area's Paiute settlements, such as rings of stone and obsidian chips. Petroglyphs (prehistoric rock carvings) found on rock outcrops in the Fish Slough area are thought to be the work of people who lived here long before the Paiutes.

The reliable presence of water in this dry country makes Fish Slough a mecca for wildlife, especially birds. Great blue herons, American bitterns, cinnamon teals, ducks, and tundra swans are just a few of the species that have been observed here. The Fish Slough area also boasts one of the highest populations of raptors in the Owens Valley, including golden eagles, prairie falcons, northern harriers, red-tailed hawks, and kestrels.

The ponds are home to several endangered animal species: the Owens pupfish, the Owens tui chub (another fish), and the Fish Slough snail. The small (up to 1.5 inches long) Owens pupfish thrives in warm, saline water. It was abundant in Owens Valley swamps, marshes, and ponds before drainage and water diversions destroyed most of the valley's natural wetlands in the 1920s and 1930s. It was considered extinct until rediscovered at Fish Slough in 1964.

The wetlands of Fish Slough support water-loving plants such as cattails, rushes, and willows. Several endangered plant species grow here, including Fish Slough milk vetch, discovered in 1974 by local botanist Mary DeDecker. Fish Slough and thousands of acres adjoining it in the Volcanic Tableland are classified as an Area of Critical Environmental Concern by the Bureau of Land Management. An interagency task force has developed long-range plans to enhance Fish Slough's environ-

mental quality, protect its rare species, and provide interpretive facilities.

Volcanic Tableland: A place of solitude and vast, high-desert panoramas, the Volcanic Tableland encompasses pinyon-juniper woodlands, cactus- and sage-covered mesas, and colorful formations of Bishop tuff. There are several unpaved roads through the tableland, making possible a two- to three-hour loop trip starting in Bishop. Consult a reliable road map (Inyo National Forest map) for routes, and stay on the main roads unless you are equipped with a 4-wheel-drive vehicle.

• *Much of the road to Fish Slough is bumpy and dusty. It has changed little since the late 1800s, when it served as the main stage route between Bishop and the mining camps of Bodie and Aurora. From Bishop, drive north on U.S. Highway 6 for 1.5 miles and bear left on Five Bridges Road. Continue 2.5 miles to a three-way junction. The right fork leads to Fish Slough, 3 miles ahead. The waters of Fish Slough emerge near the base of a 300-foot-high fault scarp that runs along the east side of the marsh. The middle fork at the three-way junction leads to Casa Diablo, a granite peak rising through the tuff in the heart of the **Volcanic Tableland**. The left fork heads west to Chalk Bluff, following Owens River and eventually connecting with U.S. 395 near Pleasant Valley Reservoir.*

The spring-fed ponds of Fish Slough, a high-desert oasis that is home to several endangered species of fish and plants. BILL EVARTS

Fireweed and granite boulders, Rock Creek Canyon. DAVID MUENCH

Rock Creek

From its headwaters in a glacial cirque, Rock Creek meanders through meadows, tumbles past stands of aspen and Jeffrey pine, and cascades through a steep gorge, dropping more than 6,000 feet on a 20-mile journey to join Owens River. Rock Creek Canyon is known for majestic scenery and year-round recreation. The upper reaches of the canyon offer cross-country skiing in winter, challenging lake and stream fishing in season, and alpine hiking and climbing in summer. Rock Creek Canyon is radiant during autumn, when willows and quaking aspens paint the slopes gold and yellow.

Little Lakes Valley: Rock Creek Canyon contains the highest roadend in the Sierra Nevada: Mosquito Flat, elevation 10,250 feet. From the roadend, an easy day hike leads into the John Muir Wilderness and the sparkling blue lakes and wildflower-carpeted meadows of Little Lakes Valley. Little Lakes Valley is a broad glacial trough set in an amphitheater of 13,000-foot peaks. The five-mile round-trip hike along the Morgan Pass Trail to scenic Long Lake provides a rewarding introduction to the Eastern Sierra high country.

Rock Creek Lake: A favorite for families and anglers, this picturesque lake in upper Rock Creek Canyon

is to drive 23 miles north of Bishop (or 0.8 miles south of Toms Place) and turn west off U.S. 395 at Swall Meadows/ Lower Rock Creek Road. It is also accessible by taking the Pine Creek/ Rovana/Lower Rock Creek exit, 9.5 miles north of Bishop on U.S. 395; make an immediate right turn onto Lower Rock Creek Road—the old highway up Sherwin Grade—and continue north about 10 miles to Lower Rock Creek Canyon.

Top: Cycling at Swall Meadows near Lower Rock Creek. JOHN MOYNIER
Bottom: Nordic skiing, upper Rock Creek Canyon. JOHN MOYNIER

offers lakefront camping and fishing for good-sized trout. A pack station is located nearby, as is a lakeside resort with its small store, restaurant, and cabin accommodations.

Lower Rock Creek: In spring or late fall, when higher elevations may be snow-covered, Lower Rock Creek Canyon makes a splendid day-hiking destination. Watch for water ouzels, western tanagers, beaver, and the occasional rattlesnake while hiking here. A trail follows Lower Rock Creek below the Swall Meadows/Lower Rock Creek Road turnoff from U.S. 395. This creekside path is accessible at a bridge located 1.9 miles down the road from the turnoff; it follows the west side of the creek through delightful Jeffrey pine forest before rejoining the road after one mile. Beyond this point, the trail continues down a dramatic river gorge that joins Owens Valley north of Bishop. This last section, however, is a long hike that requires a shuttle arrangement for your return. For further information on hiking in Lower Rock Creek, contact the White Mountain Ranger Station in Bishop.

• To reach **Rock Creek** and the trailhead for **Little Lakes Valley**, drive 24 miles north of Bishop on U.S. 395 and exit to the west at Toms Place onto Rock Creek Road. Drive 9 miles up the canyon to **Rock Creek Lake**; the roadend at Mosquito Flat/Little Lakes Valley is 3 miles farther. **Lower Rock Creek** is accessible from two directions. The quickest way to reach Lower Rock Creek

Above: Looking east across Crowley Lake, Long Valley, and the Volcanic Tableland to the crest of the White Mountains. BILL EVARTS
Opposite: McGee Canyon, a classic U-shaped glacial valley, bounded by several metamorphic peaks. FRANK BALTHIS

Crowley Lake

Grand scenery and great fishing combine to make Crowley Lake one of the most popular destinations in the Eastern Sierra. This 5,000-acre reservoir on the upper Owens River in Long Valley is flanked by the Sierra Nevada, Glass Mountain Ridge, and the Volcanic Tableland. A mecca for anglers, Crowley Lake also attracts bird watchers who come to view wintering bald eagles, migrating white pelicans, and numerous species of waterfowl and shorebirds. Sage grouse, known for their colorful courtship displays, are often observed near Crowley Lake.

Long Valley is a caldera—a large basin created in the aftermath of a volcanic explosion. The caldera was formed about 700,000 years ago following a series of immense eruptions that spewed ash as far away as present-day Nebraska. Bishop tuff, the pink to orange rock deposited by the eruptions, covered the landscape in all directions. Examples of Bishop tuff can be observed in many areas near Long Valley, including the Volcanic Tableland southeast of Crowley Lake, Owens River gorge below the lake, and the Aeolian Buttes south of Mono Lake.

During the Pleistocene, Long Valley held a lake, and an ice-age river many times the size of today's Owens River flowed from its outlet, cutting a deep gorge through the Volcanic Tableland. When pioneers arrived in the 1860s, the ice-age lake had long vanished, and Owens River meandered lazily through the meadows of Long Valley.

In 1903, the newly created Reclamation Service proposed building a dam in Long Valley to supply irrigation water to Owens Valley farmers. The reclamation plans were abandoned in 1906 after the City of Los Angeles purchased extensive land and water rights along Owens River, eventually including property in Long Valley. In 1941 Los Angeles built the Long Valley Dam to help capture additional water for the Los Angeles Aqueduct. The reservoir is named in honor of the Eastern Sierra's beloved traveling priest, Father J. J. Crowley, who endeavored to help Owens Valley residents overcome their bitterness following the "water wars" with Los Angeles.

McGee Canyon: McGee Canyon lies just west of Crowley Lake. The four-mile drive into the canyon offers marvelous vistas of Crowley Lake, the Long Valley caldera, and the distant White Mountains. McGee Creek Road crosses huge glacial moraines and climbs over the 50-foot-high Hilton Creek fault scarp, located at the west end of the McGee Creek Campground. Beyond the pack station and roadend, a trail heads upstream to the John Muir Wilderness, beckoning visitors to further explore this glacier-scoured canyon.

• *The* **Crowley Lake** *turnoff is on U.S. 395, 28.5 miles north of Bishop, or 11.5 miles south of Mammoth Junction (395/203). The McGee Creek Road exit is 31 miles north of Bishop, or 9 miles south of Mammoth Junction, and enters* **McGee Canyon** *just west of the highway.*

Mammoth Region

Winding through the rocky defiles and waterless hollows of this ancient lava field we suddenly emerge upon the green, boggy flats of Long Valley, dotted with thousands of horned cattle and veined with mazy streams shining in the sun like strips of silver.... Along the northern margin of the valley we find the volcanic forces still active and manifested in numerous hot springs, geysers and solfataras, ranged around the lava bluffs that bound the valley on the north. Here, too, the wild landscapes are indescribably sublime. The Sierra [is] on the left, [White] Inyo Mountains on the right, a purple tableland between, with lofty volcanic cones rising beyond, colored red and blue and ashy gray

—*John Muir,*
San Francisco Daily Evening Bulletin, *1875*

Left: Crimson columbine. DENNIS FLAHERTY
Opposite: Twin Lakes and the Mammoth Crest.
LARRY ULRICH

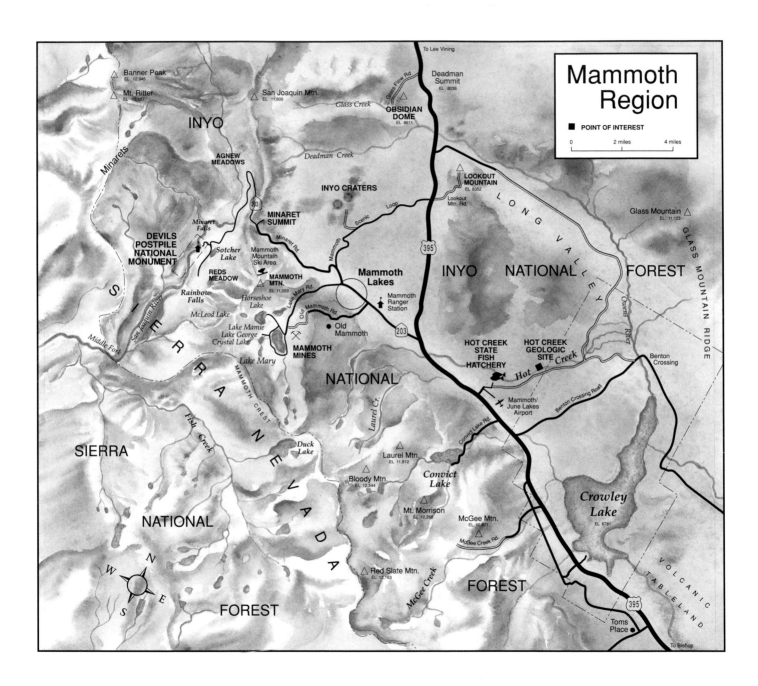

Looking across the crystal-clear waters of Convict Lake toward Sevehah Cliff. JEFF GNASS

Convict Lake

A short detour off U.S. 395 takes you to beautiful Convict Lake. This large, clear-blue lake is cupped in a glacial basin and surrounded by colorful metamorphic cliffs and peaks. The sheer walls of Mount Morrison (12,268 feet) jut skyward near the south side of the lake, displaying nearly 5,000 feet of vertical relief. Convict Lake is a highly scenic and tranquil destination, but its name is derived from a "Wild West" incident that involved a prison break, man-hunt, and shoot-out. Convict Lake was also the scene of tragedy in February 1990; seven people were drowned—three teenagers and four would-be rescuers—after falling through the lake's thin cover of ice.

The incident that resulted in the naming of Convict Lake occurred in September 1871, after 29 inmates escaped from the Nevada State Penitentiary in Carson City, Nevada. Six of the men headed south, and along the way they murdered a young mail rider from Aurora, Nevada whom they mistook for one of their former prison guards. Posses from Aurora and Benton pursued the six desperados, eventually cornering them in Monte Diablo Cañon (now Convict Canyon). Benton merchant and posse member Robert Morrison, for whom the peak is named, was killed in the ensuing gun battle. The convicts managed to fight their way out of the canyon, but they were apprehended by citizens near Bishop 10 days later. On the way back to the penitentiary in Carson City, two of the outlaws were lynched.

Little remains at Convict Lake to remind us of this frontier episode; today, visitors come to picnic, hike, fish, camp, or observe some of the area's outstanding geological features. Extensive glacial moraines spill out of the canyon mouth immediately east of the lake. Metamorphic formations near the lake contain some of the oldest rock in the Sierra Nevada; tiny fossils found in ridges near the base of Mount Morrison are estimated to be 500 million years old.

A path hugs the south shore of Convict Lake, passing metamorphic rock imbedded with ancient fossils. Another trail rounds the northern shore, follows Convict Creek through a deep glacial valley (use caution at the creek crossing), and continues up-stream to Lake Mildred, 4.5 miles from the trailhead. Look for light-colored fossils in the dark rock along the streambed.

• To reach **Convict Lake***, turn west off U.S. 395 at Convict Lake Road, 3.5 miles south of Mammoth Junction (395/203) or 1 mile north of Benton Crossing Road. The road continues 2.5 miles to the south end of the lake. In winter, Convict Lake Road is regularly cleared of snow.*

Hot Creek Geologic Site. DENNIS FLAHERTY

Hot Creek

Hot Creek churns past colorful seeps, sky-blue hot springs, and roiling clouds of steam, delighting visitors with a dynamic display of geothermal action. The creek rises at a series of springs just west of the Hot Creek State Fish Hatchery and flows east to Owens River. As it traverses Long Valley, Hot Creek enters a gorge and encounters a series of fumaroles (gas vents) and thermal springs. The springs and fumaroles on Hot Creek are thought to be heated and pressurized by an immense pool of magma (molten rock) that lies five to eight miles beneath the valley floor. This geothermal activity is concentrated along a two-mile stretch of stream, and it can be viewed at Hot Creek Geologic Site, where a short trail provides access to an overlook and observation bridge.

Hot Creek and the springs that feed it embrace a rich aquatic community, including two species of native fish: Owens tui chub and Owens sucker. Hot Creek also supports a thriving population of rainbow and brown trout and is a well-known "catch-and-release" fly-fishing stream. The area is frequented by many species of birds: dippers and spotted sandpipers feed in the creek's shallow rapids, cliff swallows build nests in the cliffs above the stream, and numerous waterfowl stop here during annual migrations.

Although pools at Hot Creek Geologic Site may appear enticing to swimmers, entering the water can be dangerous and is not recommended by the Forest Service, which administers the site. Rapid fluctuations in Hot Creek's geothermal activity can produce scalding-hot water that suddenly enters the creek. Keep dogs leashed and children carefully supervised.

Hot Creek State Fish Hatchery:

Hot Creek State Fish Hatchery is the largest hatchery in the Eastern Sierra, annually raising about three million trout for planting in Sierra Nevada lakes and streams. The hatchery also produces over 20 million eggs each year for shipment to trout-rearing facilities throughout California. Freshwater springs provide the hatchery with water that has the ideal temperature (56° to 58° F) for breeding trout. During summer, the Forest Service offers weekly interpretive tours of the hatchery; check with the Mammoth Ranger Station for a schedule. Hot Creek State Fish Hatchery is open to the public year-round from 8 a.m. to 4:30 p.m. daily.

• *To reach **Hot Creek**, exit east off U.S. 395 near the north end of the Mammoth/ June Lakes Airport, 3 miles south of Mammoth Junction (395/203). A sign reading "Fish Hatchery" marks the turnoff. Head east for about 1 mile and follow the signs to **Hot Creek State Fish Hatchery**. Continue 2.5 miles on gravel road (subject to winter closure) to the parking area for **Hot Creek Geologic Site,** open sunrise to sunset only.*

Trout fishing on the Owens River in Long Valley. JIM STROUP

Mammoth backcountry, from the 10,790-foot summit of Duck Pass. CHRISTOPHER TALBOT FRANK

Mammoth Lakes

The Mammoth area features breath-taking scenery and a cornucopia of year-round recreation. Some of the best alpine skiing in California is found at Mammoth Mountain, the most popular resort in the Eastern Sierra. Mammoth is also a delightful summer destination. Since the turn of the century, pine-shrouded Mammoth Lakes Basin has been attracting summer visitors who come for activi-ties such as fishing, hiking, and camping. The town of Mammoth Lakes offers a good range of lodging and restaurants and sponsors cultural and sporting events throughout the year.

Like many communities in the Eastern Sierra, Mammoth was initially settled by miners. The town's name—there is no "Mammoth Lake"—is taken from the historic Mammoth Mine on Red Mountain east of Lake Mary. The first Mammoth-area settlements were Mammoth City and Pine City, ramshackle mining camps that grew up in response to the 1877 gold strike on Red Mountain. Although most of the mines were shut down and the camps abandoned by 1881, a few residents remained to operate a sawmill in Mineral Park that produced lumber for the growing community of Bishop, 40 miles to the south. Mineral Park is known today as Old Mam-moth. (Historic Mammoth mining areas are covered in "The Mammoth Mines" section of this chapter.)

By the turn of the century, Mam-moth was attracting summer tourists. Its first resort hotel, the Wildasinn, opened in 1905. Mammoth was strictly a summer resort until 1927, when Tex Cushion, a French-Canadian, began providing winter transportation by dogsled between Mammoth and U.S. 395. By the late 1930s, simple ski tows were operating at several locations in the Eastern Sierra, attracting a growing number of winter vacationers to the Mammoth area. With the construction of Highway 203 in 1937, businesses relocated from Old Mammoth to an area along the new highway that became the downtown section of Mammoth Lakes. Old Mammoth is now a residential area south of the business district.

Mammoth Mountain straddles a low stretch in the Sierra Nevada crest

where moisture-laden Pacific storms move up the San Joaquin River drainage and funnel eastward over the range. As a result, Mammoth Mountain receives more snow than any place in the Eastern Sierra—an average of 335 inches per year. This fact was not lost on early-era winter sports enthusiasts, including ski pioneer Dave McCoy, who began operating a portable ski tow on Mammoth Mountain in 1941. After an all-weather road was built to the slopes and a double chairlift was installed in the mid-1950s, Mammoth Mountain quickly developed into one of California's most popular ski resorts.

Mammoth Mountain: Today, the Mammoth Mountain Ski Area comprises 3 day lodges, 30 lifts, and over 3,500 acres of ski terrain. In summer or during ski season, ride the Ski Area gondola to the top of pumice-covered Mammoth Mountain (11,053 feet) for an exhilarating view of the Sierra Nevada, Mono Craters, Mono Lake Basin, and the White Mountains. A short distance south across the top of this dormant volcano is a scenic viewpoint overlooking Mammoth Lakes Basin. Guided nature hikes are conducted here in summer by Ski Area staff. A popular hike begins at the summit, descends the east ridge of the mountain, passes the unusual rock formation known as "Hole-In-The-Wall," and ends at Twin Lakes. During summer, a shuttle bus returns hikers to the Ski Area parking lot.

Mammoth Lakes Basin: Located immediately south of Mammoth Mountain, the glacier-carved Mammoth Lakes Basin is dotted with lakes and cloaked with a forest of lodgepole pine and red fir. The basin's five major lakes— Twin Lakes, Lake Mary, Lake Mamie, Lake George, and Horseshoe Lake—range in elevation from 8,540 feet to 9,008 feet. The basin offers resort lodging and Forest Service campgrounds; swimming is permitted in Horseshoe Lake only.

Mammoth Lakes Basin is a fabulous area for day hiking. Trails from Horseshoe Lake lead to Lake McLeod or Mammoth Pass (9,290 feet). From Coldwater Campground near Lake Mary, a trail passes through a lovely lake basin, ascends Duck Pass (10,790 feet), and eventually connects with the John Muir Trail. From Lake George, there are easy hikes to T. J. and Barrett Lakes. A more strenuous 1.5-mile hike takes you from Lake George to beautiful Crystal Lake at the base of Crystal Crag.

Accessible by vehicle, Twin Falls tumbles 300 feet over an abrupt rim of volcanic rock between Lake Mamie and Twin Lakes. Overlooks along upper Lake Mary Road provide fine views to the north and east. In winter, an extensive trail system is maintained by the ski touring center at Twin Lakes, and cross-country skiers enjoy roads and trails throughout the Mammoth Lakes Basin.

Mammoth Lakes: The town of Mammoth Lakes hosts a wide range of year-round cultural activities, including concerts, an arts festival, and a crafts fair. Sporting events in the Mammoth area include world-class bicycle races, canoe racing, and a triathlon; the town also sponsors tennis, water skiing, and volleyball tournaments. The Mammoth Ranger District Visitor Center provides trail and weather information, schedules of ranger-guided tours, wilderness permits, brochures, maps, and books.

• *Begin your visit to the* **Mammoth Lakes** *area with a stop at the Mammoth Ranger District Visitor Center, located on the north side of Highway 203 about 3 miles west of U.S. 395. The town center of Mammoth Lakes is a few blocks farther west. To reach* **Mammoth Mountain Ski Area,** *turn north (right) at the intersection of Highway 203 (Minaret Road) and Lake Mary Road in Mammoth Lakes. To reach* **Mammoth Lakes Basin,** *go west (straight ahead) on Lake Mary Road at the above intersection. Drive 2.5 miles on Lake Mary Road to Twin Lakes; Lake Mary is 1 mile farther. Follow the main road around the north rim of Lake Mary to Lake Mamie, Twin Falls, and Horseshoe Lake. A signed left fork just north of Lake Mary takes you to Lake George; this same road also loops back around the south and east shores of Lake Mary, passing a turn-off to Coldwater Campground before rejoining the main Lake Mary Road.*

Above: Mammoth Mountain's exciting alpine skiing. LARRY ULRICH
Opposite: The Mammoth area receives more precipitation than any other part of the Eastern Sierra and as a result, supports dense coniferous forests like this one south of Lake Mary. CHRISTOPHER TALBOT FRANK

Top: *The well-preserved ruins of the Mammoth Consolidated Mine on Red Mountain above Lake Mary.* BILL EVARTS
Bottom: *Mill City's flywheel, an enduring remnant of the 19th-century Mammoth Mines era.* LONDIE PADELSKY

The Mammoth Mines

During the 1860s and 1870s, decades before Mammoth first became known as a summer resort, prospectors scoured the countryside near Pumice (Mammoth) Mountain in search of the legendary Lost Cement Mine. This widely publicized site was reputedly littered with cement-like gold-bearing ore. Although the Lost Cement Mine was never rediscovered, gold and silver were found on the northern slope of Red Mountain in 1877. This strike set off a vigorous but short-lived mining boom and stimulated permanent settlement in the Mammoth area.

In July 1878, Civil War veteran and mining investor General George Dodge made his way to Mammoth City, the largest of several mining camps in the Red Mountain area. When Dodge arrived, about 20 firms were working local claims, and over 1,500 people were living in area camps. For $10,000, Dodge purchased one of the most promising claims, the Mammoth Mine, and incorporated the Mammoth Mining Company. Dams were built at Lake Mary and Twin Lakes to supply hydro power for the Mammoth Mine's stamp mill, located at the company headquarters of Mill City. A 1/2-mile flume diverted water to the mill, while a tram delivered ore from the mines to the mill site.

Plagued by a combination of low yields, logistical difficulties, harsh winter weather, mismanagement, and stockholder disagreements, the Mammoth Mining Company suspended operations during the winter of 1879-80; the property was sold at a sheriff's auction in 1881. Most other Mammoth-area mines folded by 1880, and the unemployed miners soon abandoned the camps. A few diehards stayed on, even after fire destroyed half of Mammoth City in November 1880.

A revival of the Mammoth Mine in the 1890s again ended in failure. No more large-scale mining was attempted in the area until 1927, when A. G. Mahan and his son Arch organized the Mammoth Consolidated Mining Company and started tunneling for gold along the western slope of Red Mountain. The mine proved unprofitable and closed in 1933. One of the owners, Arch Mahan, Jr., later opened the Red's Meadow Pack Station, a pack outfit that still operates near Devils Postpile National Monument.

Mammoth Mines Tour: You can relive Mammoth's gold mining era by taking a leisurely half-day loop trip that combines stops at the Mammoth Museum, Mill City, and two historic mining sites on Red Mountain. The following destinations are found along a route that begins at the intersection of Highway 203 and Old Mammoth Road.

Mammoth Museum: From Highway 203, turn south onto Old Mammoth Road and continue nearly one mile to a broad right curve; at the curve, turn left onto unpaved Sherwin Creek Road and follow signs to the museum. Housed in a historic log cabin on the banks of Mammoth Creek, the museum's exhibits feature old mining implements, memorabilia, and photos of early-day Mammoth. Open daily, summer months only.

Mill City: Return to Old Mammoth Road, turn left, and continue another two miles to the end of the pavement,

passing through the original resort district of Mammoth. The parking area for Mill City is located about 300 yards beyond the end of the pavement. Sheltered in a grove of trees near the parking area rests the grave of Mrs. J. E. Townsend, a miner's wife, who—as the story goes—always dreamed of owning a house with a white picket fence. She died at age 34 during the severe winter of 1881, and her husband erected a white picket fence around her grave. A 10-minute walk from the parking lot brings you to the mill's 18-foot-high flywheel.

Mammoth Mine: Continue 1/2 mile farther up Old Mammoth Road to reach the site of the Mammoth Mine and Mammoth City. Tailing piles, burned-out timbers, and caved-in mine shafts are remnants of the operation; a sturdy square foundation, thought to be part of the tramway, can also be seen. The dwellings of many Mammoth City residents were built into the hill on the north side of the road, an area now overgrown by brush.

Mammoth Consolidated Mine: From the Mammoth Mine, continue 1/4 mile farther on Old Mammoth Road, and turn left onto Lake Mary Road. Bear left at the fork just before Lake Mary, and turn left once more to enter Coldwater Campground. The short trail to the mining camp begins on the

Stamp mill, Consolidated Mine. BILL EVARTS

east side of the parking area at the upper end of the campground.

An interpretive brochure provides a self-guiding tour of the site, leading you through the company camp and mining operations. The tour visits the owner's cabin, the mine's bunkhouses, a schoolhouse, an assay office, an ore processing mill, and the mine shafts. Many of the buildings and much of the machinery are surprisingly intact. Tour brochures are available at the site or can be picked up at the Mammoth Ranger District Visitor Center. This is the last stop on the Mammoth Mines tour, and you can retrace your route or take Lake Mary Road back to town.

• *The tour of the* **Mammoth Mines** *begins at the intersection of Highway 203 and Old Mammoth Road, about 1/2 mile west of the Mammoth Ranger District Visitor Center.*

Wildflowers at Minaret Summit, looking west to the rugged Ritter Range. DAVID MUENCH

Minaret Vista

Minaret Vista sits atop a windswept volcanic ridge on the divide that separates the massive San Joaquin River drainage to the west from the Owens River drainage to the east. This is one of the few locations in the Eastern Sierra where you can drive to the very crest of the range.

Minaret Vista offers a thrilling view of the Ritter Range, a rugged, glaciated subrange of the Sierra Nevada that is crowned by the jagged Minarets and the neighboring summits of Mount Ritter (13,157 feet) and Banner Peak (12,945 feet). There are also panoramic views northwest to the backcountry of Yosemite National Park, east to Glass Mountain Ridge and the distant White Mountains, and south to Mammoth Mountain. A picnic area and the 1/2-mile Minaret Vista Discovery Trail entice visitors to savor this beautiful, high-Sierra setting.

• *From the town of Mammoth Lakes, turn north on Minaret Road (Highway 203), drive past the Mammoth Mountain Ski Area, and continue 1 mile farther to Minaret Summit. From the summit, a side road heads a short distance north to* **Minaret Vista.** *Minaret Road is closed beyond the Ski Area from approximately November to June, depending on snowfall.*

Whitebark Pine and Clark's Nutcracker

A wind-pruned whitebark pine near the summit of Mono Pass. ANDY SELTERS

whitebark pines, especially during late summer and early fall. This jay-like bird has a light gray body, distinct white markings on its black wings and tail, and a sharp, pointed beak. The bird's frequent flights and raucous *k-r-a-a* call make it highly conspicuous.

Whitebark pine and Clark's nutcracker enjoy what biologists call a "mutualistic" relationship. The whitebark's rich pine nuts provide a crucial food supply for the Clark's nutcracker, and the bird buries large quantities of the nuts in widely dispersed caches for later retrieval. Unlike most conifers, the nuts (seeds) of whitebark pine lack "wings" and cannot be dispersed by the wind. Instead, the pine relies on the nutcracker, whose numerous caches of buried whitebark seed help spread and regenerate the species.

Clark's nutcracker. RALPH CLEVENGER

Minaret Vista, Tioga Pass, and Sonora Pass are among the few locations in the Eastern Sierra where motoring visitors can observe whitebark pine, *Pinus albicaulis*. This pine is found near timberline in mountain ranges throughout the West; in the Sierra it is widely distributed at elevations between 10,000 and 12,000 feet. A hardy, slow-growing conifer, it becomes established in rocky, exposed, subalpine locations—often where no other tree species exist.

Whitebark pines generally grow 6 to 20 feet high. Buffeted by high winds and blowing snow, they often develop stooped, shrub-like, or prostrate forms; multi-trunked specimens are common. The pine's yellow-green needles are grouped in fives and clustered at the branch tips. Its one- to three-inch-long cones are purple when immature, and the tree's bark is whitish gray.

Clark's nutcracker is a mountain resident often seen near stands of

Devils Postpile /
Reds Meadow

Spectacular volcanic formations, mist-shrouded waterfalls, hot springs, wildflower-filled meadows, dense coniferous forests, and a network of pleasant hiking trails are some of the attractions that make the Devils Postpile/Reds Meadow area a rewarding destination. The journey to Devils Postpile begins on the arid Great Basin side of the range, crosses the Sierra at 9,176-foot Minaret Summit, and descends into the scenic, heavily wooded valley of the upper Middle Fork of the San Joaquin River. The evergreen forest near Devils Postpile encompasses a lush mix of vegetation more typical of the well-watered western slope of the Sierra than the dry east side.

Devils Postpile National Monument: The combined work of volcanism, glaciation, and mechanical weathering can be witnessed in the unique setting of Devils Postpile National Monument. Devils Postpile features an outstanding example of columnar-jointed lava, a volcanic formation well-developed in only a few sites in North America.

The geologic record shows that numerous lava flows occurred in this region over the last three million years. The lava that formed Devils Postpile erupted within the last 100,000 years from vents near the

present-day site of Upper Soda Springs Campground—about two miles north of the Postpile. The eruption produced a 400-foot-deep river of molten basalt that moved southward through the valley. As the lava cooled, shrank, and began to crack, temperatures deep within the lava bed were uniform enough to allow the formation of six-sided columnar joints, a mathematically ideal configuration for the release of stress within a solidifying mass. The presence of four, five-, and seven-sided "posts" within the formation indicates that conditions were not perfectly consistent within the cooling basalt. Devils Postpile is notable because the majority of its columns are hexagonal, exhibiting a degree of regularity rarely approached in similar structures around the world.

Most of the thick basalt layer that once filled the valley was scoured away during periods of glacial advance, leaving only the columns seen at the monument. The Postpile's upper surface carries the sheen of glacial polish and is grooved with parallel lines etched into the basalt by debris-laden glaciers. The talus pile at the base of the formation consists of outside columns that were dislodged by the action of freezing and thawing water in the formation's joints. Earthquakes have also sent outer columns tumbling into the pile.

Devils Postpile came within the original boundaries of Yosemite National Park. In 1905, following heavy lobbying from mining and lumber companies, Congress removed 500 square miles from the southeastern corner of the park, including Devils Postpile. Devils Postpile received little public attention until 1910, when commercial interests proposed that it be dynamited and the debris be used to build a rock-filled dam on the San Joaquin River. Champions of the Sierra Nevada, including University of California Professor (and mountaineer) Joseph N. LeConte and the Sierra Club's William Colby, received the backing of Walter L. Huber of the Forest Service and successfully petitioned President Taft and other federal officials to preserve the area in its natural state. Devils Postpile was declared a national monument by presidential proclamation in 1911; today it attracts more than 100,000 visitors annually.

An easy 15-minute walk (0.4 mile) takes you to Devils Postpile. The trail begins at the National Monument headquarters, follows the river downstream, passes through lodgepole pine and red fir forest, and arrives at the foot of the Postpile's near-vertical, 60-foot columns of basalt. A trail leads to the top of the formation, where you can observe the hexagonal jointing of the columns and get a close look at the glacial polish atop the Postpile.

Rainbow Falls: From Devils Postpile, a two-mile hike downstream leads to Rainbow Falls, where the San Joaquin River drops 101 feet over a cliff of basalt. At midday, sunlight refracted by an ever-present cloud of mist creates a brilliant rainbow that arches across the falling river. Rainbow Falls can also be reached by a 1.5-mile hike from Reds Meadow.

Opposite: Devils Postpile. LARRY ULRICH
Above: The San Joaquin River plunges over a basalt cliff at Rainbow Falls. CARR CLIFTON

A short hike up the John Muir Trail leads to the base of Minaret Falls. DENNIS FLAHERTY

Minaret Falls: Glorious in early summer, Minaret Falls are reached by following the John Muir Trail 1/2 mile north from the National Monument headquarters. Minaret Falls Campground, located a short distance north of the Monument entrance, offers a good view of the falls.

Reds Meadow: Reds Meadow, famous for its annual display of summer wildflowers, is named after Red Sotcher who built a cabin here in 1879. Warm-water springs are piped into a public bathhouse at the meadow, and a campground, resort, pack station, and several trailheads are located nearby. The John Muir Trail passes through Devils Postpile National Monument and crosses the road near Reds Meadow, one of only two locations where this 212-mile-long wilderness trail intersects a road. The Pacific Crest Trail, which extends 2,620 miles from Mexico to Canada, joins with the John Muir Trail through most of the Sierra, including the stretch through Devils Postpile to Reds Meadow.

Sotcher Lake: The self-guided Sotcher Lake Nature Trail makes a 1.25-mile loop around this small lake located 1/2 mile north of Reds Meadow. The nature trail passes a recent avalanche path, a beaver dam, and a lagoon filled with pond lilies.

Agnew Meadows: The meadow is named after Tom Agnew, a miner who settled here in 1877 and later served as a guide for the U.S. Army troops who administered this area when it was part of Yosemite National Park. The 1/2-mile Agnew Meadows Wildflower Walk passes a variety of summer-blooming wildflowers, including monkshood, larkspur, shooting star, and meadow pensten-mon. Campgrounds, a pack station, and wilderness trailheads are also located at Agnew Meadows.

• *To reach the Devils Postpile/Reds Meadow area, turn north onto Minaret Road (Highway 203) at the intersection of Highway 203 and Lake Mary Road in the town of Mammoth Lakes. You will reach Agnew Meadows 8.5 miles west of town; Devils Postpile National Monument is 5 miles beyond Agnew Meadows, and Reds Meadow is 1 mile past the National Monument entrance. From about November to mid-June, the road to the Devils Postpile/Reds Meadow area is closed by snow. During the busy summer months, day-use visitors are required to take a shuttle bus into the area. The bus service operates seven days a week from the main parking lot at Mammoth Mountain Ski Area.*

The Mammoth-Mono Volcanic Region

Volcanism has played a major role in the geologic history of the Mammoth-Mono region, and dramatic evidence of volcanic activity can be observed throughout the area. A 30-mile-long strip between Mammoth Mountain and Mono Lake is one of the youngest volcanic regions in the United States. Scientists estimate that 20 volcanic eruptions have occurred here in the last 2,000 years—some as recently as the late 1800s.

Four sites—Inyo Craters, Lookout Mountain, Obsidian Dome, and Mono Craters Vista—provide a fascinating introduction to the Mammoth-Mono volcanic landscape. The Inyo Craters and Obsidian Dome are among a group of craters and lava domes that extend along a 10-mile-long fault system where magma (molten underground rock) has risen through weak zones in the earth's crust. This area is sometimes referred to as the Inyo Volcanic Chain and is geologically associated with the larger Mono Craters that rise a few miles to the north. Lookout Mountain, a dome that lies just east of the Inyo Volcanic Chain, offers sweeping vistas of the region's volcanic formations. The Mono Craters Vista overlooks a chain of volcanic domes and coulées (block-like or stubby, solidified lava flows) south of Mono Basin.

These destinations are situated in the rolling, forested country northeast of Mammoth Lakes. Visit them individually or explore all four in the course of a leisurely half-day tour. A Forest Service brochure provides an excellent self-guiding auto tour of 10 Mammoth-Mono area geologic sites. Titled "Craters • Cones • Coulées," the pamphlet can be used to supplement the following text and is available at the Mammoth Ranger District Visitor Center.

Inyo Craters: The Inyo Craters were formed during the Inyo Eruption, a volcanic event that took place about 600 years ago. These two funnel-shaped craters are each 600 feet in diameter; the southern crater is about 200 feet deep, and the northern crater about 100 feet deep. Melted snow and rainwater collect to form a small lake at the bottom of each pit. A 1/4-mile walk through a lovely stand of Jeffrey pine leads to the craters and a shaded picnic area.

The Inyo Craters were created by phreatic eruptions—explosions of steam and rock generated when groundwater came in contact with rising magma and became superheated. The resulting steam burst violently to the surface. Ascending magma often produces lava domes and flows, but in this case superheated groundwater created the explosion pits, and the magma remained well below the surface.

Lookout Mountain: This rounded peak, technically called a resurgent dome, was uplifted after Long Valley caldera collapsed following a series of

The Inyo Craters, known as "explosion pits," were formed during a volcanic eruption about 600 years ago. BILL EVARTS

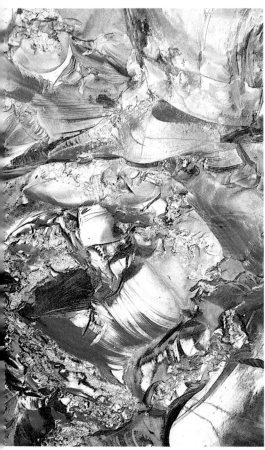

Obsidian at Panum Crater in the Mono Craters.
WILLIAM NEILL

colossal volcanic eruptions 700,000 years ago. The pink rock throughout the vicinity is Bishop tuff from the Long Valley eruption. The mountain-top (8,352 feet) offers a magnificent 360° panorama of the Mammoth-Mono region. The elliptical basin of Long Valley caldera stretches southeast to Crowley Lake and the Volcanic Tableland. Glass Mountain Ridge and the distant White Mountains fill the skyline to the east and southeast. To the north are the austere volcanic domes of the Mono Craters.

To the west and northwest you can easily detect the brown obsidian flows and craters of the Inyo Volcanic Chain; San Joaquin Ridge and the sawtooth spires of the Minarets lie beyond them. To the southwest is Mammoth Mountain, a volcano (now dormant) formed by repeated extrusions of lava between 50,000 and 200,000 years ago. Three glaciated Sierra Nevada peaks rise to the south: Bloody Mountain, Laurel Mountain (with a curving glacial moraine at its base), and the sheer face of Mount Morrison.

The surface of Lookout Mountain is sprinkled with two forms of volcanic glass: obsidian and pumice. Although identical in chemical composition, obsidian and pumice are the products of different types of volcanic extrusions. Pumice is formed when magma is explosively ejected, filling the lava with tiny air bubbles; this usually occurs during the early stage of a volcanic eruption. Obsidian is formed when viscous, molten lava flows to the surface and instantly hardens.

Obsidian Dome: This lava dome is a 300-foot-high, mile-long hill of volcanic glass, the largest of several such formations in the Inyo Volcanic Chain. Although some of the domes may be 5,000 years old, geologists believe that Obsidian Dome was part of the more recent Inyo Eruption. Obsidian domes are formed when thick, slow-moving lava oozes to the surface through a volcanic vent. Cooling too rapidly to allow mineral crystals to form, the lava hardens to obsidian. Glassy debris accumulates around the dome as additional lava pushes through the vent and cracks the cooled surface rock.

The Paiutes used obsidian to make spearheads, arrowheads, and knives. It was also an important trade item; obsidian from the Eastern Sierra was used by tribes throughout the country. Near the parking area at Obsidian Dome, you can clamber through the rubble to a short, sheer cliff of shiny obsidian. Be careful of loose, sharp rocks.

During winter, the Forest Service maintains a cross-country ski trail on Glass Flow Road to Obsidian Dome.

Mono Craters Vista: The Mono Craters comprise a group of overlap-

The lava domes of Mono Craters, one of the youngest volcanic regions in the country. JOHN S. SHELTON

ping lava domes, coulées (lava flows), and craters built up by repeated volcanic extrusions that began at least 40,000 years ago. The most recent eruption in this chain occurred about 600 years ago. Like other volcanic formations in the area, the Mono Craters are composed of rhyolite, a light gray, fine-grained rock that has the same chemical composition as granite. The craters are mined for pumice, which is used for a variety of industrial products; they are the only commercial source of pumice in the United States.

• Begin your tour of the **Mammoth-Mono Volcanic Region** at Mammoth Lakes or at Mammoth Junction (395/203). Since vehicles can easily get stuck in the loose volcanic soils found throughout the Mammoth-Mono volcanic area, stay on paved and maintained dirt roads when driving.

To reach **Inyo Craters** from the town of Mammoth Lakes, take Minaret Road (Highway 203) to Mammoth Scenic Loop, turn right, and continue 2.7 miles east. Turn left (north) at the Inyo Craters sign and continue on an unpaved road a little over 1 mile to reach the parking area and

trailhead. An alternate route begins on U.S. 395. Drive 5 miles north from Mammoth Junction, turn left on Mammoth Scenic Loop, and continue 3 miles to the Craters' signed turnoff.

To reach **Lookout Mountain** from the Inyo Craters, return to Mammoth Scenic Loop, turn left, and drive to the junction of U.S. 395. Continue straight across U.S. 395 to Lookout Mountain Road. Head east on this unpaved road, bear left at a fork after about 1 mile, and continue to the top of Lookout Mountain. To reach **Obsidian Dome**, return to U.S. 395, continue 6 miles north, and turn west on Glass Flow Road, just beyond Deadman Summit. Follow the signs 1.5 miles to a parking area. To reach **Mono Craters Vista**, return to U.S. 395, head north, continue 2 miles past June Lake Junction (395/158), and exit at West Portal Road. Head east 0.7 mile to the viewpoint. (From Lee Vining, West Portal Road is about 7 miles south on U.S. 395.)

Storm clouds over Mammoth Mountain, a dormant volcano. KATHY MEYER FLAHERTY

Mono Lake/Bridgeport Region

T he Lake, though bitter as the Dead Sea, is yet translucent as
Tahoe, and in calms mirrors the colors of its shores and the
massive cumuli that pile themselves in the purple sky above it
as no fresh water lake ever can. . . .

Nowhere within the bounds of our wonder-filled land are the antago-
nistic forces of fire and ice brought so closely and contrastingly together.
The volcanic phenomena are so striking we seem to be among the very
hearths and firesides of nature, yet standing among drifting ashes, and
turning to the mountains we behold huge moraines sweeping from the
shadowy jaws of cañons out into the basin, marking the pathways of
scores of glaciers that crawled down the mountain sides.

—John Muir,
San Francisco Daily Evening Bulletin, 1875

*Left: Aspen leaves and pine needles on the forest
floor.* DENNIS FLAHERTY
*Opposite: Mono Lake, tufa formations, and the
Mono Craters.* LARRY ULRICH

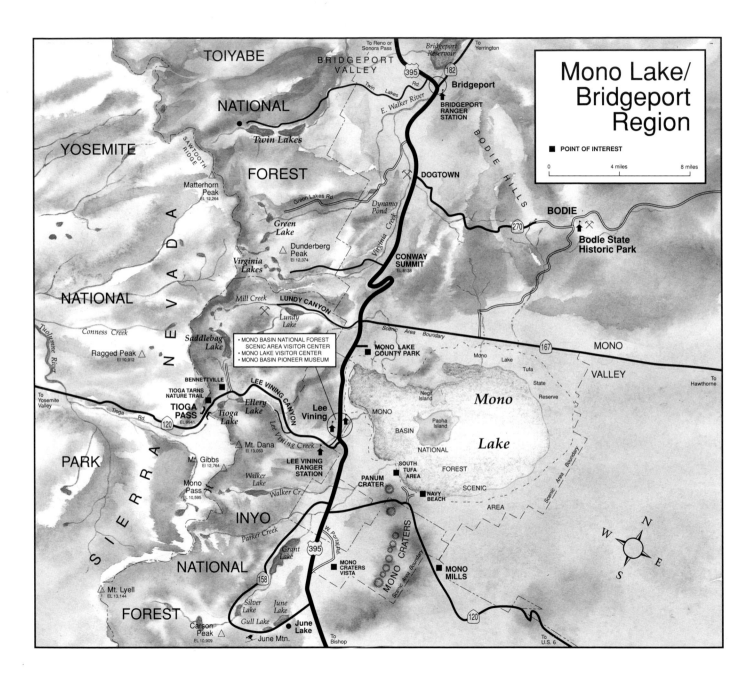

Mono Lake/ Bridgeport Region

■ POINT OF INTEREST

0   4 miles   8 miles

TOIYABE

To Reno or Sonora Pass

Bridgeport Reservoir

To Yerrington

NATIONAL

BRIDGEPORT VALLEY

Twin Lakes Rd.

395

182

Bridgeport

YOSEMITE

E. Walker River

BRIDGEPORT RANGER STATION

FOREST

Twin Lakes

BODIE HILLS

DOGTOWN

Green Lakes Rd.

Matterhorn Peak
El 12,264

Dynamo Pond

BODIE

270

Green Lake

Virginia Creek

△ Dunderberg Peak
El 12,374

Bodie State Historic Park

Virginia Lakes

CONWAY SUMMIT
EL 8138

NEVADA

Mill Creek

LUNDY CANYON

Conness Creek

Lundy Lake

NATIONAL

Scenic   Area   Boundary

MONO

• MONO BASIN NATIONAL FOREST SCENIC AREA VISITOR CENTER
• MONO LAKE VISITOR CENTER
• MONO BASIN PIONEER MUSEUM

■ MONO LAKE COUNTY PARK

VALLEY

167

Ragged Peak △
El 10,912

Saddlebag Lake

Tuolumne River

Mono Lake

Tufa

To Hawthorne

BENNETTVILLE

LEE VINING CANYON

Negit Island

State

TIOGA TARNS NATURE TRAIL

Ellery Lake

Lee Vining

MONO

Paoha Island

Reserve

Mono Lake

TIOGA PASS
EL 9941

Tioga Lake

BASIN

To Yosemite Valley

Tioga Rd.

120

△ Mt. Dana
El 13,053

Lee Vining Creek

NATIONAL

Mt. Gibbs △
El 12,764

LEE VINING RANGER STATION

SOUTH TUFA AREA

FOREST

PARK

Walker Lake

SCENIC

Mono Pass
El 10,595

PANUM CRATER

Walker Cr.

■ NAVY BEACH

AREA

Scenic Area Boundary

INYO

Parker Creek

W Portal Rd.

MONO CRATERS

N

NATIONAL

Grant Lake

395

MONO CRATERS VISTA

Scenic Area Boundary

■ **MONO MILLS**

W

E

158

S

Mt. Lyell △
El 13,144

Silver Lake

June Lake

120

FOREST

Carson Peak △
El 10,909

Gull Lake

☆ June Mtn.

June Lake

To Bishop

To U.S. 6

June Lake Loop

Nestled in a basin beneath the massive granite ramparts of 10,909-foot Carson Peak, the resort area of June Lake has long been a favorite retreat. The June Lake Loop is a delightful byway that passes through the town of June Lake and skirts each of the basin's four lakes: June, Gull, Silver, and Grant. Travelers venturing off U.S. 395 to drive the loop will enjoy the area's stunning scenery and appreciate the resort's relaxed, friendly atmosphere.

Although prospectors combed the area in search of gold, June Lake never experienced major mining activity. Its "lodestone" has always been clear mountain lakes and streams. During the 1920s, vacation cabins sprang up as Hollywood's élite discovered this picture-perfect haven.

Today the loop offers a variety of accommodations and is known for year-round outdoor recreation. June Mountain features alpine skiing, and the ski area's chalet at the top of the tram offers splendid views of the Sierra, Mono Lake, and Mono Craters. Excellent cross-country skiing terrain is found a few miles south of June Lake, off Glass Flow Road and elsewhere in the Deadman Summit area. In summer, fishing, water skiing, sailing, swimming, hiking, riding, and camping draw outdoor enthusiasts to June Lake, many of whom return year after year. In autumn, groves of

quaking aspen paint the June Lake Basin with radiant gold, attracting photographers and other visitors who come to enjoy this striking show of fall color.

• *June Lake Loop (Highway 158) is a 14-mile detour off U.S. 395. The south end of the loop intersects U.S. 395 about 15 miles north of Mammoth Junction (395/203), and the north end intersects U.S. 395 about 4.5 miles south of Lee Vining. Snowfall closes the northern leg of the loop in winter.*

Top: Outlet of Silver Lake, along the June Lake Loop. CHRISTOPHER TALBOT FRANK
Bottom: June Lake and Carson Peak. JIM STROUP

Above: Highway 120, which ascends the steep north side of Lee Vining Canyon (shown), is a National Scenic Byway from U.S. 395 to Tioga Pass. JIM STROUP
Opposite: The swift current of Lee Vining Creek as it passes through wooded Lee Vining Canyon. CHRISTOPHER TALBOT FRANK

Tioga Pass

The highest trans-Sierra highway, and one of the most spectacular auto routes in California, is the road over Tioga Pass (Highway 120). It climbs 3,300 feet from Mono Basin, traversing the steep north face of Lee Vining Canyon high above the cascading waters of Lee Vining Creek. The road crests at 9,941-foot Tioga Pass, eastern gateway to Yosemite National Park. Motorists crossing Tioga Pass journey past diverse scenery: sagebrush-covered desert, subalpine lakes and meadows, glacier-scoured peaks and domes, and on the descent to Yosemite Valley, dense coniferous forests. Near Tioga Pass, miles of hiking trails beckon visitors to stop

and explore the high country of the eastern Sierra Nevada.

Tioga Pass did not serve as a major trans-Sierra thoroughfare until the 20th century. Before then, most travelers heading for Mono Basin crossed the range by taking the Mono Trail, an Indian trade route about five miles to the south. Mining activity and, later, tourism led to the development of the modern-day Tioga Pass route. The name Tioga is an Iroquois Indian word meaning "where it forks."

In 1882 the Great Sierra Consolidated Silver Company financed construction of a wagon road from the western Sierra foothills to mines near Tioga Pass. Named the Great Sierra Wagon Road and later called the Tioga Road, the new route was soon discovered by tourists, soldiers, and stockmen. Ironically, three years after completion of the wagon road, the mines were shut down; no ore was ever extracted.

In 1915, Stephen T. Mather, then assistant to the Secretary of the Interior and later the first director of the National Park Service, helped purchase the Tioga Road from the successors of the mining company. Mather donated the road to Yosemite National Park, which renovated the route and linked it with a new stretch of state highway that extended from Lee Vining to Tioga Lake. The completed road ushered in a new era of trans-Sierra auto travel. Until 1961, however, when the paved two-lane highway was completed along the old road's route, the trip over Tioga Pass was considered an adventure. Today about 200,000 vehicles enter Yosemite National Park at Tioga Pass each year.

Lee Vining Canyon: Lee Vining Canyon is named after Leroy Vining, the first white to settle in the Mono Basin region. He crossed the Sierra on the Mono Trail in 1852 and later built a sawmill on the creek that now bears his name. Lee Vining Creek offers good fishing and is bordered by quiet campgrounds and large stands of aspen. Lee Vining Falls spill out of Ellery Lake and, in winter, the frozen waterfall features some of the best ice climbing in California.

Ellery Lake and Tioga Lake: Tucked at the foot of sheer cliffs, these scenic and highly accessible lakes are popular with anglers and campers.

Saddlebag Lake: Visitors will find excellent fishing and hiking opportunities at this lovely, high-country lake. During summer, a water taxi crosses to the north end of Saddlebag Lake, where trails fan out into a beautiful alpine lake basin known for brilliant summer wildflowers.

Bennettville: Two structures, including the camp's cook shack, are all that remain of this community that served as headquarters for the Tioga Mining District. You can hike to Bennettville on a high-elevation, mile-long trail that heads northwest from Junction Campground.

Tioga Tarns Nature Trail: This level, 1/2-mile, self-guiding nature walk is a good introduction to local natural history and geology. The trail begins 1/4 mile west of Tioga Pass Resort on the north side of Highway 120.

• *If you plan to travel over* **Tioga Pass** *in summer, give yourself plenty of time to enjoy the exhilarating scenery and allow for slow-moving traffic, especially when headed west into the park. Tioga Pass is usually closed by snow from November to Memorial Day. Tioga Pass and the east entrance to Yosemite National Park are located on Highway 120, 12 miles west of the U.S. 395/Highway 120 junction near Lee Vining.*

Highway 120 enters **Lee Vining Canyon,** *passing Lee Vining Ranger Station 1.5 miles west of the 395/120 junction; the exit for Lee Vining Canyon campgrounds is 1 mile farther west. The route then ascends the north wall of the canyon and passes* **Ellery Lake** *(10 miles west of Lee Vining) and* **Tioga Lake** *(1 mile farther) before reaching Tioga Pass. Just beyond Ellery Lake at Junction Campground, a partially paved road heads 2.5 miles north to* **Saddlebag Lake.**

Mono Lake

This vast, salty lake, shimmering in a desert basin at the foot of snow-clad mountains, is one of California's greatest natural treasures. The Mono Basin lies on the western edge of the Great Basin and is rimmed by sagebrush-covered hills to the north and east, volcanic domes to the south, and jagged granite and metamorphic peaks in Yosemite National Park to the west. Mono Basin offers incomparable scenery and encompasses a unique environment—one where visitors can view fanciful tufa towers, young volcanoes, huge flocks of migrating birds, and the lake's deep-blue waters.

Mono Lake is at least 700,000 years old, one of the oldest continuously existing lakes in North America. Like the Great Salt Lake in Utah and Pyramid Lake in Nevada, Mono Lake survives from the Pleistocene, when the earth's climate was colder and wetter, and huge inland seas filled valleys and basins throughout the West. Fed by runoff from tremendous glaciers, Mono Lake was 60 times its present size during the last ice age. The lake extended into present-day Nevada, and a mighty river flowed southeast from its outlet into Owens Valley. Following the last ice age— about 10,000 years ago—the massive lake began to recede and water eventually stopped flowing out of the basin. Today, the lake covers an area of about 66 square miles.

Mono Lake is naturally salty and alkaline because it has no outlet: the only way for water to leave is by evaporation. Although the water flowing into the lake from Sierra creeks carries only minute traces of alkali minerals and salts, these remain behind as water evaporates from the lake's surface; they have become highly concentrated over the thousands of years since the lake lost its outlet. In recent decades, water diversions from Mono Basin have dramatically reduced the size of Mono Lake; since 1941, when Los Angeles began diverting water from the four major creeks that feed it, lake volume has been cut in half and the water's salinity and alkalinity have doubled.

Mono Basin has been sculpted over millions of years by faulting, glaciation, and volcanic eruptions. Like Owens Valley to the south, Mono Basin dropped away from the Sierra as a result of repeated downfaulting along the base of the range. Glaciers carved dramatic canyons and deposited extensive moraines along the eastern Sierra Nevada escarpment to the west of the lake. The ancient, worn volcanoes of the Bodie and Anchorite hills rise to the north and east of the basin. Black Point, a dark, flat-topped volcano protruding from the lake's

Above: Mono Lake is a key feeding and resting station for migrating birds. LEWIS KEMPER
Opposite: Tufa "towers" protrude from the waters of 700,000-year-old Mono Lake. CARR CLIFTON

Above: American avocet, one of 80 water bird species at Mono Lake. B. "MOOSE" PETERSON
Opposite: Grasses, Mono Lake. WILLIAM NEILL

north shore, erupted underwater about 13,000 years ago and was gradually exposed as the lake's water level dropped. Mono Craters, a young chain of volcanic domes extending south from the lake, are of more recent origin. Younger still are Mono Lake's two volcanic islands, Negit and Paoha. Negit is about 1,700 years old, and Paoha dates back less than 325 years. No Mono Basin volcanoes are active at present, but the area shows ample potential for future eruptions.

Among Mono Lake's most intriguing phenomena are the tufa (pronounced "toofah") towers that are visible in many locations along the shore. Made of calcium carbonate, tufa is formed beneath the lake's surface when fresh water containing calcium enters the lake from underground springs and combines with the carbonate-rich lake waters. The calcium and carbonate combine, precipitating out as limestone, which builds up over time around the lake-bottom springs. Declining lake levels expose the tufa we see today, while new tufa continues to be formed beneath the lake's surface.

Most shoreline tufa formations were not visible until the 1940s, when Mono Lake began to drop as a result of water diversions. Many of these knobby spires are completely exposed, standing up to 30 feet high and providing dramatic evidence of the lake's former levels. The towers at the South Tufa Area are less than 500 years old. Far older tufa formations, perhaps dating back 13,000 years, are found near an ancient shoreline of Mono Lake, hundreds of feet above today's lake shore. Examples of older tufa can be seen to the north of Mono Lake along Highway 167, about 1.5 miles east of U.S. 395.

Mono Lake's brackish, alkaline waters may at first appear almost lifeless, but this is hardly the "dead sea" reported by 19th-century author Mark Twain. The lake supports a simple but astonishingly productive food chain and consequently is one of the single most important bird habitats in California. At the bottom of the food chain are microscopic, single-celled algae that thrive in the lake. The algae support two other animal species: brine shrimp and brine (or alkali) fly; both shrimp and flies reproduce in incredible numbers and provide a vital food resource for millions of water birds.

Almost 300 species of birds have been sighted in Mono Basin, including at least 80 species of water birds that flock to the lake each year. From spring through mid-summer, about 85% of the state's nesting population of California gulls remains at Mono Lake, mostly on Negit Island and small islands adjacent to it. Snowy plovers nest along the lake's eastern shore. Mono Lake is also an important migratory feeding station for Wilson's phalaropes, red-necked phalaropes, and eared grebes. These birds arrive at Mono Lake in staggering numbers: at least 140,000 phalaropes visit at the height of summer, and 750,000 eared grebes pass through Mono Basin between August and October.

Mono Basin has been inhabited for at least 5,500 years. When white settlers arrived, the basin was home to Northern Paiutes who called themselves the "Kuzedika." Each year in late summer they would make camp near the shore to gather and dry the lake's brine fly pupae, called "kutsavi." Added to breads and stews of pine-nut meal, this high-protein food was an integral part of their diet and trade economy. The Kuzedika collected kutsavi from the shores of Mono Lake up until the 1950s. The name "Mono," which was never used by the Paiutes, comes from the Yokut Indians, their western neighbors; it means "fly people" or "fly pupae eaters."

The first whites to see Mono Lake were a detachment of troopers, led by Army Lieutenant Tredwell Moore, who entered Mono Basin in July 1852. Lt. Moore's party was on a punitive expedition in search of Miwok Indians suspected of murdering three gold prospectors on the Merced River near Yosemite. In their pursuit of the Miwoks, Lt. Moore's group crossed the Sierra crest at Mono Pass and traveled northeast to the Mono Basin before returning to the west side of the range. Spurred by Moore's descriptions of the Sierra's east side and his samples of gold-bearing rock, Leroy Vining and several companions hired one of Moore's scouts as their guide and traveled to Mono Lake later that same year. The men set up camp on a stream that became known as Lee Vining Creek and began prospecting throughout the region.

Settlers began to homestead in Mono Basin in the 1860s, and for nearly three decades the prosperity of their ranching and farming operations was closely tied to the boom and bust cycles of nearby mining communities such as Monoville, Aurora, Bodie, and Lundy. Mono Basin's farms provided a crucial food supply for the thousands

Mono Lake moonrise. DENNIS FLAHERTY

of people and livestock that arrived at Bodie during the gold rush of the late 1870s. The Kuzedika, whose subsistence economy was severely disrupted by the arrival of the pioneers, began working as laborers for Mono Basin ranchers.

Mono Mills, situated on wooded slopes just east of the Mono Craters, was the site of an ambitious logging operation that exploited the area's vast stands of Jeffrey pine. In 1879, the *Rocket* steamboat began ferrying the mills' lumber and cordwood to the north shore of Mono Lake, where it was reloaded onto wagons and transported another 12 miles north to Bodie. The *Rocket* was replaced in 1882 by the Bodie & Benton Railway, a narrow-gauge line that skirted the east side of the lake on its 32-mile run between Bodie and Mono Mills.

By the turn of the century, most of the mining activity in Mono County had run its course, and Mono Basin became a quiet agricultural area known for cattle ranching and sheep grazing. As tourists began to discover the Eastern Sierra in the 1920s, lake excursions became popular and bathers hailed Mono Lake's water for its health-giving properties.

In the 1930s, Los Angeles acquired water rights to four of the seven creeks that flow into Mono Lake. The city's Department of Water and Power began diverting stream water out of the basin in 1941 and accelerated diversions with the completion of a second aqueduct in 1970. Since the 1970s, water diversion from Mono Basin has been the subject of an environmental controversy that has attracted nationwide attention. (See the sidebar, "The Battle to Protect Mono Lake.")

Mono Basin is open for year-round recreation and encompasses both the Mono Basin National Forest Scenic Area (Inyo National Forest) and the Mono Lake Tufa State Reserve (California Department of Parks and Recreation). Hiking, swimming, bird watching, and photography are some of the more popular activities for Mono Lake visitors.

Lee Vining: With two visitor centers and a history museum, Lee Vining makes a good starting point for a tour of Mono Basin. The Mono Basin National Forest Scenic Area Visitor Center, which opened in late 1991, overlooks the lake from a bluff on the north side of Lee Vining. This beautiful new facility contains exhibits, an auditorium, and a bookstore. State Park and Forest Service rangers offer summer tours and talks on a regular basis. Located in the center of town on U.S. 395, the Mono Lake Committee's Visitor Center features informative exhibits, a free slide show about Mono Lake, and a broad selection of regional literature; during summer, its staff conducts interpretive activities such as guided walks. The Mono Basin Historical Museum, next to Hess Park on the east side of town, features exhibits that chronicle the pioneer history of Mono Basin.

Panum Crater: A short trail leads to the rim of Panum Crater, northernmost volcano in the Mono Craters chain. About 640 years ago, a volcanic vent spewed out pumice and ash, forming the crater's outer ring. A subsequent eruption pushed viscous, fast-cooling lava into the crater, creating an obsidian dome and capping the vent. Successive thrusts of lava caused the dome to crack and reform several times.

South Tufa Area: This is the best destination for a visit to Mono Lake if you only have time for one stop. A self-guided tour takes you through a spectacular "forest" of tufa towers along the lake's scenic shoreline.

Navy Beach: This is the best site on Mono Lake for swimming or putting in kayaks and canoes. An easy shoreline hike leads about 1/2 mile west to the South Tufa Area. Because of unpredictable winds, stay close to shore when boating on Mono Lake.

Mono Mills: The logging community of Mono Mills grew up around a sawmill that operated here from 1878 to 1917. At its peak, the operation employed hundreds of loggers and laborers to harvest and mill the area's Jeffrey pine. No structures remain at Mono Mills.

Mono Lake County Park: This is a pleasant destination for bird watching, picnicking, or viewing tufa. A 1/4-mile-long boardwalk leads through a marsh to the lake shore. The park's shaded grounds offer fine views across the lake; facilities include restrooms, a picnic area, and a playground.

Conway Summit: A scenic turnout just below 8,138-foot Conway Summit—the highest point on U.S. 395—offers a superb vista of the Sierra Nevada, Mono Lake, and Mono Craters.

• *Lee Vining is just north of the inter-section of Highway 120 and U.S. 395. To reach **Panum Crater**, drive 5 miles south of Lee Vining on U.S. 395, turn east on Highway 120, go 3 miles, and turn north onto a dirt road that leads a short distance to the trailhead. To reach the **South Tufa Area** and **Navy Beach**, travel 4.5 miles east on Highway 120 from U.S. 395 and turn north at South Tufa Road. The road forks a short distance after leaving the highway; bear left for the South Tufa Area, or take the right fork for Navy Beach. **Mono Mills** is marked by a sign on the north side of Highway 120, about 9 miles east of U.S. 395. To reach **Mono Lake County Park**, drive 4.5 miles north of Lee Vining on U.S. 395, turn east on Cemetery Road, and continue a short distance to the parking area. The turnout for **Conway Summit** is 8 miles north of Lee Vining on U.S. 395.*

Autumn vista at Conway Summit, looking west to Dunderberg Peak. WILLIAM NEILL

The Battle to Protect Mono Lake

Mono Lake, focal point of one of California's greatest environmental battles. DENNIS FLAHERTY

Prior to Mono Basin water diversions—which began in the 1940s—Mono Lake's volume had been relatively stable, with inflow roughly balancing water lost to evaporation. In recent decades, however, the lake's level has dropped significantly. If water diversions are not curtailed, many biologists fear that the lake will eventually become too saline to support brine shrimp and brine flies—critical food resources for the millions of birds that visit the lake. At times, a land bridge to Negit Island has been exposed by low water levels, making sensitive California gull nesting areas vulnerable to predators. Mono Basin's expanding acreage of alkali flats—land that was formerly under water—contribute to infrequent, but severe regional dust storms. In short, Mono Lake's remarkable ecosystem may be in peril.

The Mono Lake Committee, a nonprofit citizens group, is leading the preservation effort. In 1989 the state enacted legislation directing the Committee and Los Angeles to cooperatively develop alternative water sources for the city. The outcome of lawsuits filed by the Committee and the Audubon Society may ultimately settle the issue of Mono Basin water diversions.

Here is a chronology of major events in the battle to save Mono Lake:

1978: David Gaines (1947-1988) establishes the Mono Lake Committee to help protect Mono Lake. Through the efforts of this group and others, Mono Lake receives increasing recognition for its value.

1981: California's State Legislature creates the Mono Lake Tufa State Reserve to protect the lake's unusual limestone tufa formations and fragile shoreline habitat.

1983: In response to a lawsuit filed by the Audubon Society, the California Supreme Court rules that the lake's inherent natural and recreational values should be protected.

1984: The United States Congress creates Mono Basin National Forest Scenic Area, mandating protection of the ecologic and scenic values of Mono Lake and surrounding lands.

1989: California enacts legislation whereby Los Angeles and the Mono Lake Committee can apply cooperatively for funds to develop alternative water sources in exchange for permanent protection for Mono Lake.

1989: El Dorado County Superior Court issues a preliminary injunction forcing the Los Angeles Department of Water and Power to temporarily halt Mono Basin water diversions. (This decision was reaffirmed in 1991.)

1990: The California Third District Court declares invalid Los Angeles' licenses to divert Mono Lake's tributary streams. It also requires that the streams be restored to their prediversion condition.

Beaver ponds, Lundy Canyon. WILLIAM NEILL

Lundy Canyon

Tranquil and secluded, Lundy Canyon is a wonderful area for recreational pursuits such as camping, fishing, hiking, and bird watching. Some of the Eastern Sierra's finest and most accessible displays of wildflowers are found in upper Lundy Canyon along Mill Creek. The creek tumbles out of the Sierra to feed Lundy Lake, located near the mouth of this glaciated canyon. A quiet resort on the west end of the lake occupies the former site of Lundy, a lively mining town during the canyon's gold-mining heyday in the early 1880s.

The canyon is named for William O. Lundy, who built a water-powered sawmill near the head of the lake in 1876 to supply lumber to Bodie. Prospectors discovered gold-bearing quartz in Lundy Canyon and adjacent Lake Canyon in 1879 and soon organized the Homer Mining District. Much of the mining activity was centered in Lundy Canyon about two miles west of the lake. The most profitable mines, however, were located on Mount Scowden, which towers to the south of Lundy Lake. Situated on steep, talus-covered slopes above 11,000 feet, the mines were reached by a toll road that climbed over 2,000 feet from Lundy Canyon. William O. Lundy's mine on Mount Scowden, the May Lundy, accounted for most of the estimated $1 million in gold taken from the Homer Mining District.

In 1880, Lundy had a population of 500 people, seven saloons, and two general stores. The town's popular weekly newspaper, the *Homer Mining Index*, was published by "Lyin' Jim" Townsend. In that halcyon year, the May Lundy was producing 25 tons of ore a day, stagecoaches made daily runs to Bodie, and commerce was brisk between Lundy and the Tioga Mining District to the southwest. But by 1884, the richest ore had been extracted from the mountain, the May Lundy was bankrupt, and most of the miners had moved on. Lundy's history

was further accented by thundering avalanches that took several lives and demolished structures in 1882 and 1911, discouraging attempts to maintain a year-round settlement in the canyon.

To explore Lundy Canyon, start at Lundy Lake Resort, where you will find a store and boat rentals. From the resort, a dirt road takes you about one mile farther west up Lundy Canyon. At the roadend, a moderate 1.5-mile hike leads into the Hoover Wilderness along Mill Creek, heading past beaver dams and a small waterfall before arriving at the slender, 200-foot cascade of Lundy Falls. Along with its fantastic show of wildflowers in early summer, Lundy Canyon offers vibrant displays of fall color.

• *To reach* **Lundy Lake**, *drive 6 miles north of Lee Vining on U.S. 395, turn west on Lundy Road, and continue 5.5 miles west to the lake. Lundy Road is closed by snow in winter.*

Dogtown

The discovery of gold on the western slope of the Sierra in 1848 triggered the largest westward migration in United States history. The Eastern Sierra experienced its first gold rush nearly a decade later. In 1857, miners hurried east across the range to the diggings of Dogtown, where gold placers had been found along a creek just north of Mono Basin. The ramshackle mining camp that sprang up on the site was named "Dogtown" after the miners' term for the crude housing that was typical of mining camps in the West.

Most of the miners at Dogtown abandoned the camp in 1859, lured to the promising gold placers at Monoville several miles to the south. Dogtown never yielded large quantities of gold, but this short-lived mining camp was among the first white settlements in Mono County. The ruins of rock shelters that housed some of Dogtown's miners are still visible today.

• *The roadside parking for* **Dogtown** *is located 6 miles north of Conway Summit (or 14 miles north of Lee Vining) on the west side of U.S. 395. A California State Historic Landmark sign indicates the site, which is managed by the Bureau of Land Management.*

Bodie

Bodie, the largest unrestored ghost town in the American West, sprawls across a broad, windswept valley in the hills north of Mono Lake. The mines of Bodie produced a mineral bonanza and triggered the Eastern Sierra's greatest mining stampede. Between 1877 and 1888, Bodie yielded $35 million in gold and silver—a staggering sum a century

The authentic ghost town of Bodie is now protected as a State Historic Park. LARRY ULRICH

ago. At its peak, Bodie claimed 10,000 residents, hundreds of active mining claims, and four newspapers. Bodie also developed a reputation as a lawless "Wild West" town; the mining camp was plagued by violence, and its dozens of saloons, gambling halls, opium dens, and bordellos contributed to its notoriety.

After Bodie's mines closed, most of the camp's citizens moved on. They left behind a remarkably well-preserved town, now protected within a California State Historic Park. Many of Bodie's original structures remain standing and have been left in a condition of "arrested decay." Visitors can stroll the town's streets, marvel at picturesque, weather-beaten stores and homes, and peer into windows to view abandoned merchandise, tools,

furniture, and household items that conjure up scenes from a century ago.

The town was named after William S. Bodey, a prospector who found gold placers in the Bodie Hills in 1859. ("Bodie" is said to have been a sign painter's misspelling.) Later that year, while traveling from Monoville to his Bodie diggings, he was trapped in a blizzard and froze to death. Bodey's discovery, however, stimulated the district's first wave of exploration and mining activity, attracting the support of wealthy investors such as California Governor Leland Stanford and Judge F. T. Bechtel. A notable Bodie detractor was State Geologist Josiah Whitney, who initially regarded the area as worthless. For a time his judgment held true; despite well-capitalized operations mounted by several companies, Bodie's gold proved elusive, and for 15 frustrating years the expected bonanza failed to materialize.

In 1874 two Swedish miners, Louis Lockberg and Peter Essington, bought the Bunker Hill-Bullion property, which had been first developed in 1861. Soon after they began working the claim, a section of their mine shaft caved in, exposing a rich vein of gold-bearing ore. The men crushed the rock in an arrastra, a simple mule- and water-powered mill. After two very profitable years, they sold out to a group of San Francisco investors for $75,000.

The new owners of the Bunker Hill claim established the Standard Consolidated Company, and their mine eventually became one of the largest gold ore producers in California history. By the summer of 1877, reports of the rich ore extracted at the Standard mine set off the Bodie gold rush. Packed with passengers, Bodie-bound wagons and stagecoaches arrived daily, and within a matter of months the burgeoning camp had swelled into a city of thousands, many of whom lived in tents and wood shacks.

By the winter of 1878 Bodie (8,369 feet) had developed a critical shortage of lumber, firewood, and shelter. Extensive cutting of pinyon pines near the Bodie Hills aggravated tensions with the area's Paiute Indians, who considered pinyons sacred and relied on the trees' protein-rich nuts for their winter diet. Lumber mills near Bridgeport could not keep up with the mining camp's surging demand for wood. The shortage wasn't eased until 1879, when large-scale logging in the Jeffrey pine forest south of Mono Lake began providing Bodie with much-needed lumber and cordwood.

The most profitable mining era at Bodie was short-lived, lasting less than a decade. By the late 1880s, most of the mines were closed and the population had dwindled to a few hundred people. The majority of Bodie's gold and silver came from the mines of the Bodie Company and the Standard Consolidated Company, rival operations that merged after ore production plummeted in the early 1880s.

Introduction of the cyanide gold-leaching process revitalized mining in Bodie for a few years at the turn of the century, but the town never regained its former vigor. Although Bodie survived a major fire in 1892, a more disastrous blaze destroyed most of the residential section in 1932. After its only school closed in 1940 Bodie was virtually abandoned, its buildings and homes left to the elements.

Recognized as one of the most extensive remnants of an authentic California mining town, Bodie was purchased by the State of California in 1962. It was declared a State Historic

Bodie's weather-beaten buildings date from the town's 1870-80s heyday. DAVID MUENCH

Park in 1964. The park features a self-guided walking tour, accompanied by an informative brochure. A short stroll takes you to Bodie's cemeteries, situated on a low rise southwest of town. The Miners' Union Hall, open mid-May through September, houses a fascinating museum and carries a comprehensive selection of books, maps, and brochures. During summer, tours of the Standard Mill are conducted on weekends. There are restrooms and a water fountain at

Bodie, but no stores, restaurants, or camping facilities.

Bodie State Historic Park is open from 9 a.m. to 7 p.m. Memorial Day through Labor Day, and from 9 a.m. to 4 p.m. the rest of the year. Park hours are strictly enforced. An entry fee is charged per vehicle; a fee is also charged for dogs brought into the park.

The Bodie Hills may witness yet another period of gold-mining activity. A proposal by a Canadian firm to develop a large, open-pit mine just outside the state park boundary has sparked controversy and attracted nationwide attention. Mono County officials continue to study the possible environmental effects of this proposed project.

*• Drive 7 miles north of Conway Summit on U.S. 395 and follow Highway 270 about 13 miles east to **Bodie**. The last 3 miles are unpaved. There is also a southern approach to Bodie, not suitable for RVs or trailers: from U.S. 395, take Highway 167 about 7 miles east to Cottonwood Canyon Road; turn left and continue 11 miles north on rough, unpaved Cottonwood Canyon Road to Bodie. Both routes are subject to snow closures in winter.*

Bridgeport Valley

Although eastern California claims a number of picturesque rural commu-nities, few can match the pastoral setting and magnificent scenery found near Bridgeport. Cradled between the Sierra Nevada, the Sweetwater Mountains, and the Bodie Hills, the lush pastures of Bridgeport Valley (6,400 feet) pose a striking contrast to the gray sagebrush of Mono Basin to the south. The town of Bridgeport, on the east side of the valley, is home to the historic Mono County Courthouse, the second-oldest continuously used county courthouse in California. This two-story, Italianate-style structure was built in 1880. In addition to sightseeing in town, visitors to the region should venture into one of the nearby Sierra canyons, where oppor-tunities for mountain recreation and exploration abound.

Originally known as Big Meadows, Bridgeport Valley was an important hunting and food gathering area for Northern Paiute Indians. The first white explorer to see Bridgeport Valley, frontiersman Joseph R. Walker, passed through the region during his historic crossing of the Sierra in 1833. A decade later, John C. Frémont's California-bound expedition briefly surveyed the valley, but it wasn't until the 1860s that pioneers arrived to stay. With the discovery of gold in the Eastern Sierra at Dogtown and Monoville and silver at Aurora, Nevada, settlers in the Bridgeport Valley had ready-made markets for their livestock and lumber. Bridgeport

soon became an established agricul-tural center, prospering from com-merce with the mining districts at Aurora, Lundy, Bodie, and in the early 1900s, the Masonic Mining District northeast of town.

The original seat of government for Mono County was Aurora, but when a state-funded survey determined that Aurora was located three miles inside the Nevada border, the county seat was promptly moved to California—first to Bodie and then, in 1864, to Bridgeport. Today, ranching and tourism form the backbone of the area's economy, and Mono County, where over 90% of the land is owned by public agencies, remains one of California's most pristine regions.

Bridgeport: While visitors come to Bridgeport primarily to see its courthouse and county museum, they also enjoy the community's friendly, old-fashioned atmosphere. The Mono County Courthouse, on U.S. 395, is open to the public weekdays, from 9 a.m. to 5 p.m. The Mono County Museum, located two blocks from the courthouse (next to the county park) is open summer months only, from 10 a.m. to 5 p.m. daily. Its colorful displays feature regional history, and include an especially fine collection of Paiute baskets. The Bridgeport Ranger Station, 1/2 mile south of town on U.S. 395, has information, maps, and books, as well as permits for camping and backpacking.

Virginia Lakes: Located at the edge of the Hoover Wilderness near the imposing summit of 12,374-foot Dunderberg Peak, this chain of subalpine lakes is a scenic destination for fishing, hiking, or camping. Renowned for fall color, the Virginia Lakes area (9,400 feet) also boasts a diverse array of summer wildflowers.

Green Lake: Backcountry travel to several alpine and subalpine lake basins, including the beautiful Green Lake area, begins at the trailhead at the end of Green Lakes Road. En route to the trailhead the road passes Dynamo Pond, where ruins and a plaque mark the site of a hydroelectric plant built in 1892 to supply power to Bodie. The 13-mile-long power line from Dynamo Pond to Bodie carried the first long-distance commercial transmission of electricity in history.

Twin Lakes: Sawtooth Ridge and rugged Matterhorn Peak—where small glaciers still cling to the mountainsides—form the spectacular backdrop to this popular resort area. Here boating, fishing, and camping attract thousands of visitors every summer.

Sonora Pass: Beginning in 1863, a public toll road was built over 9,624-foot-high Sonora Pass. Construction lasted five years, and the new wagon road—named the Sonora and Mono Road—became the principal thoroughfare from western California to Mono County during the gold rush to Bodie in the late 1870s. Today Highway 108 follows the route of the historic Sonora and Mono Road. Travelers headed over Sonora Pass may enjoy a stop at Leavitt Meadows, located on the Walker River a few miles east of Sonora Pass.

• **Bridgeport** is on U.S. 395, 25 miles north of Lee Vining. The **Virginia Lakes** Road heads 6 miles west from U.S. 395 at Conway Summit. **Green Lakes** Road intersects U.S. 395 about 4.5 miles south of Bridgeport, or 21 miles north of Lee Vining; Dynamo Pond is 3.5 miles up the road. Twin Lakes Road runs 14 miles southwest from Bridgeport to **Twin Lakes.** The road over **Sonora Pass,** Highway 108, begins at Sonora Junction, 17 miles north of Bridgeport. This steep, winding, two-lane route is not recommended for trucks or trailers.

Above: Late spring snow near Sonora Pass, northwest of Bridgeport Valley. BILL EVARTS
Opposite: The Mono County Courthouse, built in 1880, is still in use today. LARRY ULRICH

VISITOR RESOURCES IN THE EASTERN SIERRA

Bishop Chamber of Commerce
690 N. Main
Bishop, CA 93514
(619) 873-8405

Bodie State Historic Park
P.O. Box 515
Bridgeport, CA 93517
(619) 647-6445

**Bureau of Land Management
Bishop Resource Area**
787 Main St., Suite P
Bishop, CA 93514
(619) 872-4881

The Bureau of Land Management (BLM) manages most of the lower elevation desert areas of the Eastern Sierra. The BLM is responsible for the conservation and management of public lands. Various uses of the lands in the Bishop Resource Area include mining, livestock grazing, wilderness preservation, wildlife habitat management, and outdoor recreation. The Bishop Resource Area encompasses 750,000 acres between the Sierra Nevada range and the border of Nevada, offering recreational opportunities that include hiking, camping, mountain biking, fishing, and snowmobile and off-road-vehicle use.

The BLM is involved with several special projects in the Eastern Sierra. The agency is a partner in the management of the Fish Slough Area of Critical Environmental Concern in cooperation with the Los Angeles Department of Water and Power, California Department of Fish and Game, the U.S. Fish and Wildlife Service, and the University of California Natural Reserve System. Crater Mountain, located near Big Pine, is under study for designation as a BLM Area of Critical Environmental Concern. Brochures and recreation information are available at the Bishop office.

**California Department of
Fish and Game**
407 W. Line St.
Bishop, CA 93514
(619) 872-1171

The California Department of Fish and Game (DFG) is actively involved in maintaining the biodiversity of the Eastern Sierra by protecting habitats for aquatic organisms, amphibians, reptiles, birds, mammals, and plants. Managing fisheries in over 620 lakes and several hundred streams in the region, the DFG is responsible for aerial fingerling trout plants, roadside catchable trout programs, wild trout habitat protection, and angling regulations enforcement. Deer herds and upland game populations are managed through hunting regulations and habitat protection and enhancement.

To the Eastern Sierra visitor, perhaps the most visible work by DFG is their four state fish hatcheries which are open to the public: Mount Whitney, Black Rock, Fish Springs, and Hot Creek. Also of special interest is the work being done by DFG to monitor and promote survival of bighorn sheep and pronghorn in the Eastern Sierra.

California Native Plant Society
Bristlecone Chapter
P.O. Box 506
Independence, CA 93526

Devils Postpile National Monument
P.O. Box 501
Mammoth Lakes, CA 93546
(619) 934-2289

Eastern California Museum
P.O. Box 206
155 N. Grant St.
Independence, CA 93526
(619) 878-2411 (weekdays)
(619) 878-2010 (weekends)
Open Wednesday through Sunday from noon to 4 p.m. and on Saturday from 10 a.m. to 4 p.m.

Eastern Sierra Audubon Society
P.O. Box 624
Bishop, CA 93515

Eastern Sierra Interpretive Association
350 Inyo St.
P.O. Drawer 1088
Lone Pine, CA 93545
(619) 876-5324

The Eastern Sierra Interpretive Association (ESIA), a nonprofit organization, cooperates with the Forest Service in the distribution and sale of interpretive materials. Revenue from the sale of these items supports the historical, scientific, and educational activities of the Inyo and Toiyabe national forests, the Lake Tahoe Basin Management Unit, and the Eastern Sierra InterAgency Visitor Center. Association-produced publications include: "Bristlecone Discovery Trail," "Craters • Cones • Coulees," " Guide to Cross-Country Skiing—Inyo National Forest," and "Mammoth Trails."

Inyo National Forest
Forest Headquarters
873 N. Main St.
Bishop, CA 93514
(619) 873-5841

Attracting an estimated 11 million visitors per year, Inyo National Forest is one of the most popular National Forests in the nation. The forest's 1.9 million acres are managed primarily for recreation and wilderness preservation, but timber harvests, grazing, mining, and research are also conducted on these public lands.

Inyo National Forest offers year-round recreation, including camping, hiking, fishing, skiing, boating, and horseback riding; hunting occurs in appropriate seasons. Mountain bicycles, off road vehicles, and snowmobiles are allowed in designated areas. Six wilderness areas—Hoover, Ansel Adams (formerly Minarets), John Muir, Golden Trout, South Sierra, and Boundary Peak—totaling 552,058 acres, are found within Inyo National Forest. Other important recreation landmarks in the forest are the Mono Basin National Forest Scenic Area, Palisades Glacier, Mount Whitney, and the White Mountain's Ancient Bristlecone Pine Forest.

Besides the well known features mentioned above, Inyo National Forest includes special interest areas and facilities. Fourteen pack stations provide horseback riding access to wilderness areas. Hot Creek Recreation Area and Long Valley have significant geothermal resources. There are thousands of archaeological sites within Inyo National Forest. Research stations exist in the Ancient Bristlecone Pine Forest and at White Mountain.

Inyo National Forest Visitor Centers:

Eastern Sierra InterAgency Visitor Center
Junction of Highway 136 and U.S. 395
P.O. Drawer R
Lone Pine, CA 93545
(619) 876-4252
Open 7 days a week, 8 a.m. to 4:50 p.m.; extended summer hours.

Mono Basin National Forest Scenic Area Visitor Center
Opened in late 1991, this new visitor center is located on the north side of Lee Vining, overlooking Mono Lake.

Ranger District Offices:
(All carry books, maps, and brochures.)

Mount Whitney District
P.O. Box 8
Lone Pine, CA 93545
(619) 876-5542
Open Monday through Friday, 8 a.m. to 4:30 p.m.; extended summer hours.

White Mountain District
798 N. Main St.
Bishop, CA 93514
(619) 873-4207
Open Monday through Friday, 8 a.m. to 4:30 p.m.; extended summer hours.

Mammoth District
P.O. Box 148
Mammoth Lakes, CA 93546
(619) 934-2505
Open Monday through Saturday, 8 a.m. to 4:30 p.m.; extended summer hours.

Mono Lake District
P.O. Box 429
Lee Vining, CA 93541
(619) 647-6525
Open Monday through Friday, 8 a.m. to 4:30 p.m.; extended summer hours.

Laws Railroad Museum and Historical Site
P.O. Box 363
Bishop, CA 93514
(619) 873-5950

Lone Pine Chamber of Commerce
120 S. Main St.
Lone Pine, CA 93545
(619) 876-4444

Los Angeles Department of Water and Power
Bishop Administrative Office
873 N. Main St., Room 227
Bishop, CA 93514
(619) 872-1104

The City of Los Angeles owns approximately 312,000 acres in Inyo and Mono counties; this land is managed by the Los Angeles Department of Water and Power (DWP). Developing and protecting Los Angeles' water supply is the primary mission of DWP in the Eastern Sierra. Throughout the region, DWP maintains a complex system of aqueducts, wells, reservoirs, dams, and hydroelectric power plants.

DWP also manages rural lands that have been purchased by the City of Los Angeles to protect the Eastern Sierra watershed surrounding the Los Angeles Aqueduct System. About 90% of this city-owned land is open for day-use recreation such as hiking, fishing, boating, and hunting. (See "Owens

River" text in Chapter Six.) Some of the Eastern Sierra's more popular day-use recreation areas are located on City of Los Angeles land: Crowley Lake Reservoir, Pleasant Valley Reservoir, Grant Lake Reservoir, Diaz Lake, Klondike Lake, and portions of the Owens River. Three campgrounds on DWP land are leased to and operated by county agencies.

As a member of the InterAgency Committee on Owens Valley Land and Wildlife, DWP has been involved in a number of InterAgency projects including the Tule Elk Viewpoint, the Tule Elk Habitat Management Plan, the Off-Road Vehicle Plan, the Owens Valley Native Pupfish Sanctuary, and the InterAgency Visitor Center.

Mammoth Mountain
P.O. Box 24
Mammoth Lakes, CA 93546
(619) 934-2571

Mammoth Lakes Visitors Bureau
P.O. Box 48
Mammoth Lakes, CA 93546
(619) 934-2712

Mono County Historical Society
P.O. Box 417
Bridgeport, CA 93517

**Mono Lake Committee /
Lee Vining Chamber of Commerce**
P.O. Box 29
Lee Vining, CA 93541
(619) 647-6595

Mono Lake Tufa State Reserve
P.O. Box 99
Lee Vining, CA 93541
(619) 647-6331

Mono Basin Historical Society
P.O. Box 31
Lee Vining, CA 94541

Paiute Shoshone Indian Cultural Center
P.O. Box 1281
Bishop, CA 93515
(619) 873-4478

Sierra Club, Toiyabe Chapter
Eastern Sierra Committee
P.O. Box 406
Lone Pine, CA 93545

Southern Mono County Historical Society
P.O. Box 65
Mammoth Lakes, CA 93546

**Toiyabe National Forest
Bridgeport Ranger District**
P.O. Box 595
Bridgeport, CA 93517
(619) 932-7070
Open Monday through Friday, 8 a.m. to 4:30 p.m.; extended summer hours.

Encompassing five million acres in eastern California and western Nevada, Toiyabe is the largest National Forest in the contiguous 48 states; it is administered by the Forest Service through its multi-use management program. The northern part of the Eastern Sierra, from Sonora Pass south to Conway Summit, falls within the Bridgeport Ranger District of Toiyabe National Forest.

The one-million-acre Bridgeport Ranger District manages forest resources for recreation, wildlife, grazing, timber, and mining activities. Recreational activities offered in the Bridgeport Ranger District include hiking, riding, camping, fishing, skiing, and scenic driving. Hunting, snowmobiles, and off-road vehicles are allowed in designated areas; check with the district office.

The most notable recreation areas in the Eastern Sierra portion of Toiyabe National Forest are Bridgeport Valley, Twin Lakes, and Hoover Wilderness. Bridgeport Valley has seven National Forest campgrounds, dozens of lakes and streams, and trailheads into Hoover Wilderness. Twin Lakes offers two resorts, hiking, and fishing. A back-country trail system in Hoover Wilderness provides access to 42,800 acres of rugged mountains, alpine lakes, and rushing streams. The Bridgeport Ranger District offices contain a visitor center.

**University of California
White Mountain Research Station**
3000 E. Line St.
Bishop, CA 93514
(619) 873-4344

White Mountain Research Station (WMRS) comprises four separate lab sites at elevations ranging from 4,000 feet to 14,000 feet, and serves as a research facility for all campuses of the University of California and for dozens of other universities, colleges, and institutions. Principal goals are to support research and instruction, provide facilities for federal, state, and local groups doing research in the region, and encourage protection of the unique natural habitats of the area. The WMRS-sponsored "Fall Lecture Series" is offered without charge to the general public at the Research Station's Bishop facility, and features researchers in a variety of disciplines.

SELECTED BIBLIOGRAPHY

Arno, Stephen F. *Discovering Sierra Trees.* Yosemite: Yosemite Natural History Association and Sequoia Natural History Association, 1973.

Austin, Mary. *The Land of Little Rain.* 1903. Reprint. Albuquerque: University of New Mexico Press, 1974.

Bakker, Elna S. *An Island Called California.* Berkeley: University of California Press, 1971.

Brewer, William H. *Up and Down California in 1860-1864.* 1930. Reprint. Berkeley: University of California Press, 1966.

Browning, Peter. *Place Names of the Sierra Nevada.* Berkeley: Wilderness Press, 1986.

Cain, Ella M. *The Story of Early Mono County.* San Francisco: Fearon Publishers, 1961.

Chalfant, W.A. *The Story of Inyo.* 1933. Reprint. Bishop: Chalfant Press, 1975.

DeDecker, Mary. *Mines of the Eastern Sierra.* Glendale: La Siesta Press, 1966.

Farquhar, Francis P. *History of the Sierra Nevada.* Berkeley: University of California Press, 1965.

Fiero, Bill. *Geology of the Great Basin.* Reno: University of Nevada Press, 1986.

Fletcher, Thomas C. *Paiute, Prospector, Pioneer.* Lee Vining: Artemisia Press, 1987.

Foster, Lynne. *Adventuring in the California Desert.* San Francisco: Sierra Club Books, 1981.

Friends of the Eastern California Museum. *Mountains to Desert.* Independence: Friends of the Eastern California Museum, 1988.

Engberg, Robert, ed. *John Muir Summering in the Sierra.* Madison: University of Wisconsin Press, 1984.

Gaines, David and the Mono Lake Committee. *Mono Lake Guidebook.* rev. ed. Lee Vining: Mono Lake Committee/Kutsavi Books, 1989.

Gaines, David. *Birds of Yosemite and the East Slope.* Lee Vining: Artemisia Press, 1988.

Hall, Clarence A., Jr., ed. *Natural History of the White-Inyo Range.* Berkeley: University of California Press, 1991.

Hill, Mary. *Geology of the Sierra Nevada.* Berkeley: University of California Press, 1975.

Kahrl, William L. *Water and Power.* Berkeley: University of California Press, 1982.

King, Clarence. *Mountaineering in the Sierra Nevada.* 1874. Reprint. New York: Penguin Books, 1989.

Likes, Robert C., and Glenn R. Day. *From This Mountain.* Bishop: Chalfant Press, 1975.

Muir, John. *My First Summer in the Sierra.* 1911. Reprint. New York: Penguin Books, 1987.

Nadeau, Remi A. *The Water Seekers.* Rev. ed. Salt Lake City: Peregrine Smith, 1974.

Peattie, Donald C. *A Natural History of Western Trees.* Boston: Houghton Mifflin Company, 1953.

Reed, Adele. *Old Mammoth.* Palo Alto: Genny Smith Books, 1982.

Reisner, Marc. *Cadillac Desert: The American West and Its Disappearing Water.* New York: Penguin Books, 1986.

Rinehart, Dean C., and Ward C. Smith. *Earthquakes and Young Volcanoes along the Eastern Sierra Nevada.* Los Altos: William Kaufmann, Inc., 1982.

Sharp, Robert P. *Geology Field Guide to Southern California.* Dubuque: Kendall/Hunt Publishing Company, 1976.

Smith, Genny, ed. *Deepest Valley.* Los Altos: Genny Smith Books, rev. ed. 1978.

————, ed. *Mammoth Lakes Sierra.* 5th ed. Mammoth Lakes: Genny Smith Books, 1989.

Storer, Tracy I., and Robert L. Usinger. *Sierra Nevada Natural History.* Berkeley: University of California Press, 1963.

Trimble, Stephen. *The Sagebrush Ocean.* Reno: University of Nevada Press, 1989.

Wedertz, Frank S. *Bodie 1859-1900.* Bishop: Chalfant Press, 1969.

Whitney, Stephen. *A Sierra Club Naturalist's Guide to The Sierra Nevada.* San Francisco: Sierra Club Books, 1979.

INDEX